4RF
5

Pickles, Relishes & Chutneys

Pickles, Relishes & Chutneys

Gail Duff

Tastes, traditions and 60 international recipes,
with notes on their origins and uses

CHARTWELL BOOKS, INC.

A QUARTO BOOK

Published by Chartwell Books
A Division of Book Sales, Inc.
114 Northfield Avenue
Edison, New Jersey, 08837

This edition produced for sale
in the U.S.A., its territories
and dependencies only.

ISBN 0-7858-0352-1

This book was designed and produced by
Quarto Publishing Plc
The Old Brewery
6 Blundell Street
London N7 9BH

Art Director: Moira Clinch
Design: Design Revolution
Art Editor: Liz Brown
Copy Editor: Jackie Matthews
Home Economist: Mandy Phipps
Picture Researcher: Susannah Jayes
Picture Manager: Giulia Hetherington
Senior Editor: Sian Parkhouse
Editorial Director: Mark Dartford
Photographers: Paul Forrester, Laura Wickenden

Typeset in Great Britain by Central Southern Typesetters, Eastbourne
Manufactured in Hong Kong by Regent Publishing Services Ltd
Printed in China by Leefung Asco Printers Ltd

Contents

≈

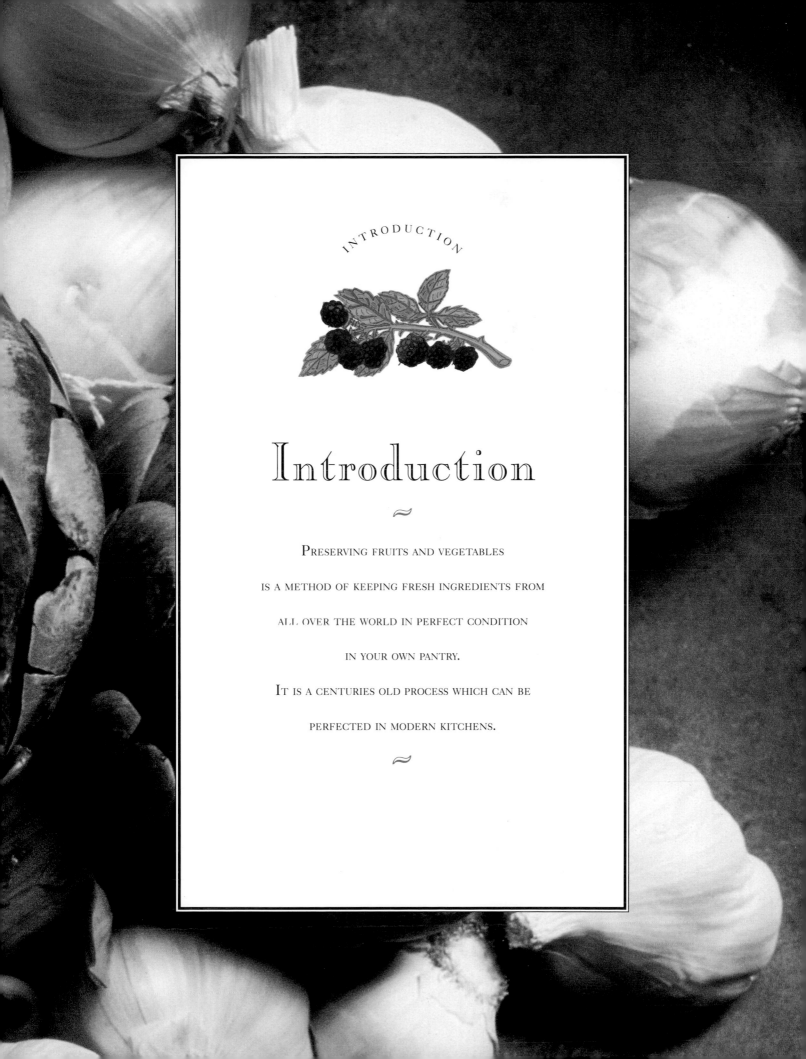

INTRODUCTION

Introduction

≈

PRESERVING FRUITS AND VEGETABLES

IS A METHOD OF KEEPING FRESH INGREDIENTS FROM

ALL OVER THE WORLD IN PERFECT CONDITION

IN YOUR OWN PANTRY.

IT IS A CENTURIES OLD PROCESS WHICH CAN BE

PERFECTED IN MODERN KITCHENS.

≈

INTRODUCTION

~

*PRESERVING MAKES EXCELLENT USE OF FOODS PRODUCED IN THEIR
NATURAL SEASON AND HARVESTED IN PERFECT CONDITION. BUT IT IS NOT MERELY A MATTER
OF ECONOMY, CATCHING PRODUCE AT ITS PEAK, WHEN PLENTY MEANS CHEAP, FOR USE LATER
IN THE YEAR. IT IS ALSO ABOUT ENJOYMENT. NATURALLY SUN-RIPENED VEGETABLES AND
FRUIT, FOR EXAMPLE, CAN TASTE FAR BETTER PRESERVED THAN THE SAME BASIC FRESH
INGREDIENTS FORCED TO GROW OUT OF SEASON IN WEAK LIGHT. MOREOVER, PRESERVING IS
A FORM OF ALCHEMY, A MARVELOUS TRANSFORMATION OF BASIC INGREDIENTS INTO
SOMETHING ENTIRELY DIFFERENT, EXCITING, AND DELICIOUS.*

*Since early times, sprigs of
herbs have been put into
the pickle jar for both
appearance and flavor.
Dill has always been one
of the most popular of
pickle herbs, and both
its feathery leaves
and its seeds are used.
It can be used with a
range of summer
vegetables but is best
of all with cucumber.*

*Boxes full of summer's
bounty, the perfect
ingredients for pickles and
chutneys. Here are sweet
bell peppers of all colors
to be pickled alone or with
other vegetables, tomatoes
for chutneys and
cauliflowers to give a
crunch to Piccalilli.*

Before the advent of freezers, where much of our surplus garden produce ends up, other methods of keeping harvested vegetables and fruits before they spoiled had to be devised. The drying of fruit is no doubt the oldest form of preserving fruit, but the technique of making pickles out of vegetables and fruits was already well known thousands of years ago.

The ancient Egyptians, Greeks, and Romans, as well as the Celts, certainly knew all about how to alter the flavor and texture of vegetables by pickling them. During the Dark Ages the practice was carried on in the monasteries, subsequently flowering in medieval times, when it became an art learned by the mistress of every house. In the

sixteenth and seventeenth centuries, when new ingredients were discovered in foreign lands and brought to Europe, the cookbook, containing recipes for preserves, became a valued item in many home kitchens. Trade with India introduced chutneys and relishes to Europe, especially Britain, adding an important extra dimension to savory preserving.

The early recipes, made in English country kitchens and preserving rooms, have changed very little over the years. Although they have been slimmed down and simplified, the basic methods and end results remain the same. In fact, the wheel seems to have come full circle. In the seventeenth century, for example, cooks seemed willing to pickle just about anything that was edible and ready to absorb influences from all over the world. But by the middle of the twentieth century, the English at least seemed to have limited their interest in savory preserves to pickled beets, red cabbage, onions, and cucumbers, many of which were commercially produced rather than prepared at home. But that is all changing now.

Today, the world is a much smaller place and many countries are more cosmopolitan. Ethnic communities have introduced their foods to alien cultures, and supermarket shelves and market stalls all over the world offer exotic fruits and vegetables to be

*Plants of the genus Solanum, which are all
related to the potato and nightshade. They
include the tomato which, although at first
treated with suspicion in the West, became one
of the most popular ingredients for making
pickles, chutneys, and sauces.*

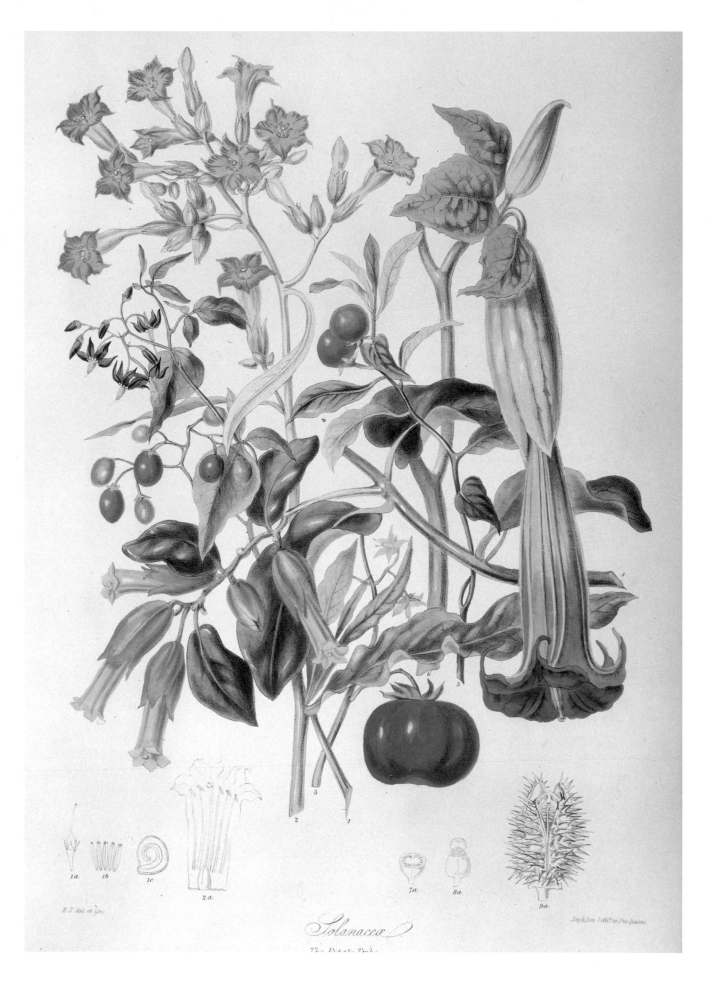

Solanaceæ

The Potato Tribe.

Spicy pickled mushrooms flavoured with ginger

Red-wine vinegar: perfect for making pickles with red-colored and robust-flavored ingredients such as red cabbage and beets, or red-colored fruits such as raspberries, cherries or plums. Buy the best-quality vinegar you can afford.

experimented with. Gardening catalogues feature new baby vegetables. We now take far more interest in new foods and in the recipes of other countries than at any time since the seventeenth century.

Combine these with our old favorites and the possibilities for creating new savory preserves are limitless.

The time is right to start pickling again and to make new chutneys and relishes. But what exactly are savory preserves, and what is the difference between them? For many people, the words "pickle," "chutney," and "relish" have become somewhat interchangeable, which is not surprising as many manufacturers' labels are equally confused. In culinary terms, however, there are clear differences between these three types of preserve which are all based on vegetable or fruits.

Pickles can be made with vegetables or fruits. Vegetables are usually salted, either with dry salt or brine (a salt and water solution), before being packed into jars and covered with a spiced vinegar. Various flavorings such as herb sprigs or spices can be put into the jars. Fruits are usually poached in a spiced vinegar syrup. Pickles are clear and the vegetables and fruits remain recognizable. Vegetable pickles are eaten while they are still crisp.

Chutneys are made from mixtures of chopped vegetables and fruits mixed with vinegar, sugar, and spices that are simmered for a long time until they reach the consistency of jam. They keep well over a long period during which their flavors improve and mellow.

Relishes are made in different ways all over the world. Many are rather like a cross between a pickle and a chutney, made from finely chopped and salted vegetables cooked very quickly in a vinegar mixture before being bottled. Some of these cooked relishes are thickened with flour or cornstarch. Others are mixtures of puréed raw vegetables and herbs. Some raw ones contain yogurt, others are

cooked with a small amount of vinegar.

No matter where they are from or when they are used, pickles, chutneys, and relishes are always an excellent extra ingredient that will complement or improve the flavor of any main dish, be it a plain roast, a curry, kebabs, tortillas, or hamburgers. Their basic ingredients are very similar and most are based on fresh, occasionally dried, vegetables and fruits with the addition of salt, vinegar, oil, sugar, and spices in varying proportions. There are so many different combinations and preparation methods that nearly every country in the world has its own characteristic recipes.

HOMEMADE PRESERVES

The best of these savory preserves are homemade but there is a lot more to home preserving than simply preparing food that is good to eat. Preserving foods in our own kitchens for the use of our family and friends keeps us in touch with the traditions of past cooks and gardeners. When working through the different stages of preparation, and maybe even growing the basic ingredients in the garden, think how many other cooks, down through so many centuries, have done exactly the same thing as you are doing.

Preserving at home also puts us in touch with the year's natural cycle, something that so many people living in cities have forgotten about. Living in heated houses and apartments and going to stores that sell the same frozen produce all the year-round, it is easy to lose track of the passing seasons. But when you take an interest in preserving you will soon learn which fruits and vegetables are best at which times of the year, for even the imported ones have their seasons. Summertime will come to mean tomatoes and soft fruits and winter time citrus fruits and roots. This may not seem relevant today, but at one time our lives were governed by the solstices and equinoxes, by the passing of the seasons and the phases of the moon. To recognize the wheel of the year is important for every person, no matter how you do it.

A selection of vinegars and spiced pickled fruits. Choose pickle jars that are both atttractive and practical. Spices for clear pickles can be tied in small pieces of cheesecloth so they can be lifted out easily and do not spoil the appearance of the pickle.

Pickles, relishes, and chutneys in history

~

WE HAVE INHERITED A GREAT LEGACY

OF RECIPES AND METHODS FOR MAKING

PICKLES AND CHUTNEYS.

THE FIRST PICKLES WERE MADE

ABOUT TEN THOUSAND YEARS AGO AND

METHODS AND INGREDIENTS HAVE BEEN

IMPROVING EVER SINCE.

~

PICKLES, RELISHES, *and* CHUTNEYS *in* HISTORY

~

As soon as people started to grow and farm their own food, it became necessary to find ways of preserving any surplus for the lean times, and it was probably about 10,000 years ago that it was discovered acids, sugars, salt, and alcohol have preserving properties. How these worked was not understood until the end of the nineteenth century, but the fact that they did was all that mattered in the early years of civilization. Immersing food in one or a mixture of these basic ingredients, is, after drying, the most ancient method we have of preserving fruit and vegetables.

Cabbages have been used for pickles since Roman times when a recipe was devised for pickling the stems. During the medieval period, the whole cabbage was shredded and pickled and went under the name of "pickled greens."

As soon as the fermentation process of liquids was discovered, probably accidentally, acids and alcohol became available, the acids at first being the result of unsuccessful attempts to produce alcohol. Sour wine, or the equivalent, was probably the first pickling medium. There was not any sugar in those early times, so honey was the main luxury sweetening ingredient and it was soon found that food swamped in honey would be exceptionally well preserved. Salt was mined in some areas and produced by panning (evaporating sea water) around the coasts.

It is known that the ancient Egyptians pickled many food ingredients between 3000 and 1000 B.C. The Celts used vinegar and were probably responsible for spreading its use throughout Europe and into Britain. The Greeks made some pickles, but it was the Romans who became skilled in the process and developed recipes that formed the basis of later knowledge. Many of their ingredients were imported from all over the Roman Empire: vegetables from Europe and fruits such as lemons, peaches, and apricots from Africa, the Middle East, and Spain. These were used alongside homegrown herbs, roots, and flowers.

Roman pickles were based on a brine of vinegar and salt mixed with olive oil, on wine must (a by-product of wine fermentation), and sometimes on pure honey. They were sealed in large, cylindrical earthenware jars and kept for considerable periods of time, sometimes even buried in the garden to ensure an even, cool temperature.

Roman vinegar was actually sour wine, and the French origin of the English name for it, "vin aigre," means just that. Sometimes yeast, dried figs, salt, and honey were added to it to make a preserving liquid. The same liquid was also watered down and used as a drink, the same one that the New Testament records as being used at Christ's crucifixion.

Two Roman writers, Apicius and Columella, have left us recipes for a wide variety of pickles, including lettuce leaves, turnips, asparagus, fennel, onions, cabbage stems, and

In the late-nineteenth century bought pickles and chutneys became popular, along with bottled sauces and bottled fruits. A wide selection could be bought from grocers' stores.

Bombay, on the Malabar Coast of India, which, in the seventeenth century, belonged to the East India Company of England. From here, spices and other ingredients for pickles, such as mangoes and limes, were exported.

plums. Columella wrote in the first century A.D. that "vinegar and hard brine are essential for making preserves," a statement that still applies to pickles today.

When the Roman Empire collapsed in the fifth century A.D., sophistications such as food preservation and pickle making were in danger of disappearing from the Western world. Fortunately, some preserves continued to be made in the monasteries where the monks grew their own food and constructed special rooms for its preparation and preservation. The rest of the population were too preoccupied with obtaining and defending land to be concerned with preserving vegetables.

CULINARY ARTS REVIVED

It was not until the eleventh century, when domestic life began to quiet down again, that the more gentle of the culinary arts began to be revived. Most European large medieval houses had their own garden and some had orchards, but the range of vegetables grown was fairly small, consisting mainly of cabbages, root crops, leeks, and onions, plus a selection of herbs.

Cabbages, first mentioned as "pickled greens" in a household list of 1290, appear to have been a regular ingredient for pickling. Wine, vinegar, and verjuice (the sour juice of

crab apples and, in later years, unripe grapes) were the main pickling liquids. Fruit was still preserved in a honey syrup or by drying.

Pickles were, as they are now, recognizable chunks of vegetable preserved in a liquid. Finely chopped mixtures of vegetables cooked to a purée with preserving ingredients were rare, although a book written by Goodman of Paris in 1393 includes a recipe for something called "compost," consisting of walnuts, turnips, carrots, pears, pumpkins, peaches, fennel, and Hamburg parsley roots simmered with a large mixture of spices in quantities of wine. As it took four months to make it was probably not very popular, certainly not in the average manor house which grew only everyday vegetables.

The types of vegetables and fruits available increased during the sixteenth and seventeenth centuries as seafarers went farther afield and returned with their botanical discoveries. Mushrooms, which had been viewed with suspicion during medieval times, became one of the most popular of pickling ingredients, along with walnuts, various wild plants, salad vegetables, and flowers, the latter making attractive edible garnishes for salads. Great care was taken when pickling rosebuds, for example, to ensure that they kept their bright color. Brilliant red or orange nasturtium buds were also a favorite at this time, when the decoration of food was almost an art form. Pickled vegetables were also both garnish and part of a dish. They were served with fresh vegetables, in salads and also with cooked vegetables to add a contrast in flavor. Verjuice was frequently used at this time which probably gave the pickles a much milder flavor than those of later years which were based on vinegar.

Increasing numbers of cookbooks appeared during the seventeenth century, and works by Gervase Markham, Robert May, and John Evelyn all contain a considerable number of pickle recipes. Evelyn, writing in 1699, gives in detail recipes for diverse ingredients such as artichoke hearts, ash-keys, green beans, broom buds, elder buds, cauliflowers, cowslips, cucumbers, lemons, melons, mushrooms, radish pods, the small green fruits of the potato plant (which we would now consider poisonous), purslane, samphire, and walnuts.

By the end of the seventeenth century, the increase in British trade with the East India Company had introduced many new ideas and ingredients to Europe from India, among them

When the Roman Empire fell apart, the art of pickling and preserving was carried on in the monasteries. The monks were almost completely self-sufficient and the sharp condiments were a welcome addition to a frugal diet.

A string of fresh onions, one of the earliest ingredients to be pickled and still just as important today as it ever was

Wine vinegar, when it could be obtained, was the favorite liquid for pickling, along with wine itself and grape juice which had just begun to ferment but not yet become wine. The quality of the malt vinegar available commercially was very poor and many cooks in country houses made their own.

By this time, Europeans had pushed west into North America, settled, and established farms and gardens. Farmhouses on the east coast had special buildings for dairying, pickling, and preserving. They also had big root cellars where all kinds of vegetables and fruit, such as potatoes, squashes, pumpkins, and apples, were stored. Down among the fresh produce were dried corn and beans and jars of pickles.

EIGHTEENTH-CENTURY RECIPES

In Britain, more cookbooks were appearing and most included special sections on preserving and pickling. Hannah Glasse's 1774 book contained modern-sounding recipes for onions, beets, red cabbage, and gherkins alongside the Elizabethan descendants of concoctions for asparagus, fennel, artichoke hearts, radish pods, and samphire. Her main pickling liquid is wine vinegar which suggests that toward the end of the eighteenth century, pickles became more pungent and vinegary, more, in fact, as they are today. She also used large quantities of the savory spices such as mustard seed and ginger, and horseradish, but did not have any recipes for chutney.

No matter what the pickling process, the color of vegetables immersed in vinegar or brine for a certain length of time will always fade slightly. The attempt to prevent this happening led to the eighteenth-century vogue for using copper salts after it was discovered that if they were added to the vinegar, vegetables kept their green color.

USE OF COPPER PANS

Using copper pans, which reacted with the vinegar, had the same effect and these processes were often specifically called for in early cookbooks. The habit was eventually called into disrepute by Elizabeth Raffald who published *The Experienced English Housekeeper* in 1782. She informed her readers that using artificial greening methods was "poison to a great degree" and advocated the strict adherence to "following strictly the direction

mangoes, chutney, and ketchups. The Hindustani word "chatni," signifying a strong, sweet relish, was very soon Westernized and has been used ever since for the thick, stewed concoctions of vinegar and vegetables.

European cooks very soon copied the chutneys and Indian-style pickles. One of the first of these new-style recipes was what we now know as Piccalilli, which first appeared in a cookbook of 1694 under the heading "To pickle lila, an Indian pickle." Because mangoes were imported into Britain already pickled, the name mango was as often used for the pickles as for the fruit itself. From John Evelyn onward, recipe writers "made a mango" of a variety of vegetables and fruits. Evelyn's recipe, a "Mango of Cucumbers," is rather like a typically English cucumber pickle of the time with a little mustard added. Marrows, melons, peaches, plums, and even apples were all in their time made into "mangoes."

Throughout the eighteenth century, plain meats served with an increasing variety of pickles and chutneys replaced the old-style meals of meats in sauces. More fruits were put into pickles than before, among them red currants, grapes, and barberries. Tomatoes were used for the first time. Finally accepted as a vegetable they were made into a sour pickle with garlic, ginger, and vinegar.

of your receipts for any kind of pickles ... greened only by pouring your vinegar hot upon them, and it will keep a long time." She included over thirty pickle recipes in her book (cucumbers, walnuts, mushrooms, barberries, nasturtiums, elder shoots, and radish pods were still popular, as were cauliflowers, beets, and grapes), but there were still none for chutney.

THE NINETEENTH CENTURY

Moving on into the nineteenth century, *The Cook's Oracle*, published in 1822, made some excellent suggestions for making pickles, most of which are still relevant today. The instructions for spiced vinegar and the advice on the types of jars that should be used (not glazed earthenware or the lead will leach out) could, with only a few changes, be put into a modern cookbook. The actual recipes are for walnuts, gherkins, beets, onions, red cabbage, cauliflower, and Piccalilli, a very much refined and modernized list compared with Elizabeth Raffald's recipes forty years earlier.

Later in the nineteenth century, the English Victorian recipe writers Eliza Acton and Mrs. Beeton gave one recipe each for "Chetney Sauce." Both recipes were said to have come from India, Mrs. Beeton's specifically from Bengal, and both were based on apples and raisins, although Eliza Acton's also contained tomatoes, which were becoming increasingly popular for ketchups and sauces. Neither recipe was actually a cooked chutney, though. Eliza Acton's ingredients were pounded in a mortar, mixed with spices and vinegar, and bottled uncooked. Mrs. Beeton's were chopped, mixed with vast quantities of salt and spices, put into a jar, and covered with vinegar. After a month both "chetneys" were strained and bottled, with the vinegar being reserved separately as an addition to cooked sauces. Eliza Acton recommended using a "good genuine vinegar, French or English," or a good-quality homemade one.

In the late-nineteenth century, quite a variety of commercially made pickles became available, the most popular eventually being beets, onions, red cabbage, and walnuts.

Households, however, had begun to make their own chutneys and relishes based on the original Indian recipes. In Victorian times it became the norm, when it could be afforded, to have hot roast meat on Sundays and to save

enough to be eaten cold on several of the following days. Plain cold meat is not necessarily very appetizing which is why chutneys and relishes became so appealing. Making chutney–chopping the ingredients, and stewing them with vinegar and spices– was in a way a less precise process than pickling. Chutneys could also be made of mixtures of ripe ingredients. Consequently, they became increasingly popular in ordinary households, especially in country districts where there were often surpluses of vegetables throughout the summer.

Because the ingredients of a chutney very often depended upon availability at the time of making, there were few, or perhaps even no classic recipes. As a result, very few chutney recipes were ever written down. You are more likely to find favorite recipes in your grandmother's hand-written recipe book than you are in a published work of the time. Chutney making was a very personal thing. You could learn a basic method and then go your own way.

Chutneys keep well, they are easily potted and are often sold at country bazaars and on market stalls. For the past two hundred years, alongside jam, they have been the mainstay of the country cook's pantry. Relishes were often quickly made on the spur of the moment, again, using any ingredient that seemed appropriate and available. They kept for only a short time and then were forgotten. The old cookbooks do not contain any relish recipes at all. The history of pickles stretches back over thousands of years, while chutneys and relishes are relatively modern upstarts. All together, however, these tasty preserves have come to epitomize the country store, the thrifty use of surplus vegetables, and fruits for times of shortage, and the magic of creating new, wonderful flavors to enhance ordinary foods.

In the early part of the twentieth century commercially prepared pickles became available. H. J. Heinz was one of the leading manufacturers.

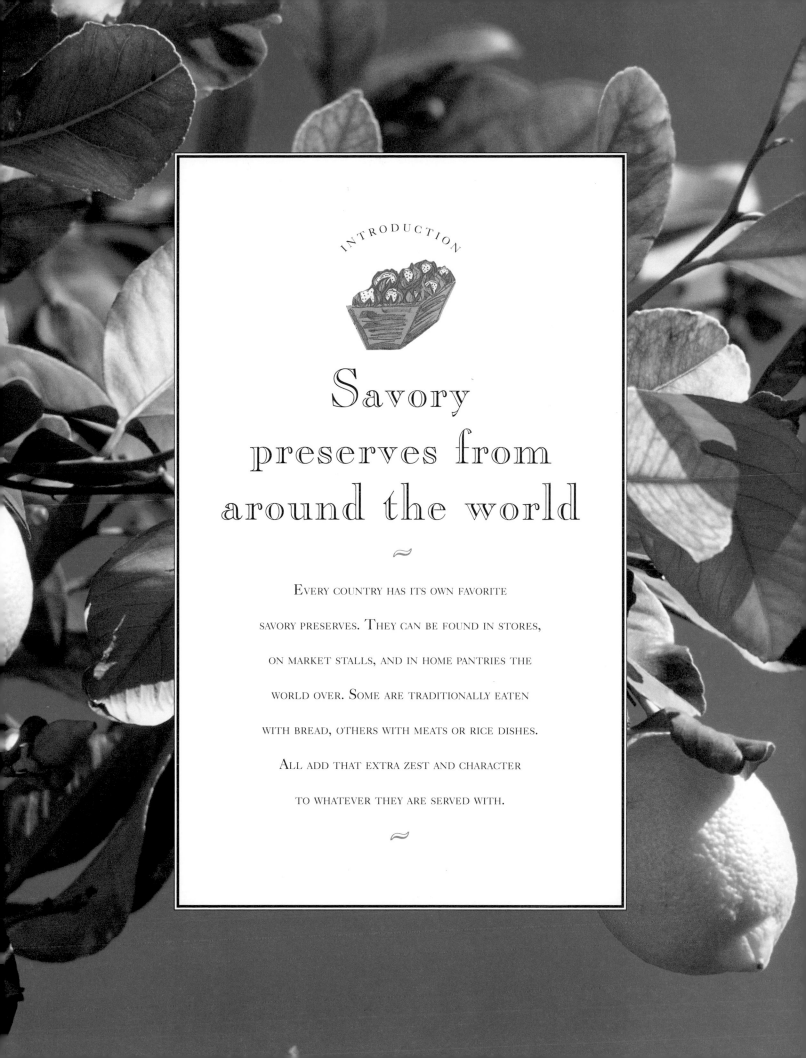

INTRODUCTION

Savory
preserves from
around the world

~

EVERY COUNTRY HAS ITS OWN FAVORITE

SAVORY PRESERVES. THEY CAN BE FOUND IN STORES,

ON MARKET STALLS, AND IN HOME PANTRIES THE

WORLD OVER. SOME ARE TRADITIONALLY EATEN

WITH BREAD, OTHERS WITH MEATS OR RICE DISHES.

ALL ADD THAT EXTRA ZEST AND CHARACTER

TO WHATEVER THEY ARE SERVED WITH.

~

SAVORY PRESERVES *from* AROUND *the* WORLD

~

PICKLES, CHUTNEYS, AND RELISHES ARE FOUND ALL OVER THE WORLD.
THEY RANGE FROM THE HUMBLE, HOMEMADE APPLE CHUTNEYS SOLD AT ENGLISH
VILLAGE FAIRS TO THE EXOTIC, SHREDDED GREENS PRESERVED IN RICE WINE THAT YOU
MAY FIND GARNISHING CHINESE DISHES OF MEAT, FISH, OR RICE. THERE ARE MANGO
CHUTNEYS IN THE CARIBBEAN, SHARP DILL PICKLES IN EASTERN EUROPE, PICKLED
RED ONION SLICES IN MEXICO, AND QUICKLY MADE YOGURT RELISHES IN INDIA.
ALL ENHANCE OR COMPLEMENT THE MAIN DISHES THAT THEY ACCOMPANY.
MANY ARE ONLY EVER MADE IN THE HOME.

It is not known for sure who first discovered how to preserve surplus foods in this way, but certainly it was a practice already well known in the Middle East by 3000 B.C. Methods of preparation in the region have changed very little over the centuries, and today many small, specialist food stores have large jars filled with a wide variety of colorful pickled ingredients that the proprietor or his family have prepared. Pickles are also sold from the jar by street vendors, to be eaten instantly with flat Arab bread which is dipped in the vinegar. When the jar is empty, the vinegar is sold for use at home as a basis for sauces and to liven up rice dishes.

The art of pickle making is usually learned at home and many families pride themselves on their well-stocked pantry, crammed with rows of jars in which every conceivable vegetable has been immersed in pickling liquid to be served either as an accompaniment, as a snack with bread, or in place of a salad. These Middle Eastern pickles are made in a fairly standard way. The raw or slightly cooked vegetables or fruits, which are sometimes salted first, are packed into sterilized jars and covered with a cold liquid. This may be pure vinegar and salt, a mixture of vinegar and salt water in varying proportions, or a good-quality oil. Great care is taken to dislodge any

The eggplant, or aubergine, is a frequent ingredient in Middle Eastern pickles, either alone or with mixtures of peppers, cucumbers, cauliflower, baby onions, and artichoke hearts.

air bubbles from the jars which are then tightly sealed. It is a simple process but very effective and the strength and saltiness of the liquid determines the ultimate flavor and keeping qualities of the pickle. In the main, the mixture of the vinegar with water makes Middle Eastern pickles milder than those made with pure vinegar in Western countries. Herbs such as dill, garlic, hot chili peppers, and a variety of spices may all be added for extra flavor.

The most-popular vegetables for Middle Eastern pickles are sweet bell peppers and hot chili peppers, eggplants, either whole or sliced, cucumbers, cauliflowers, turnips, baby onions, okra, and artichoke hearts. These can be used singly or in mixtures known as *titvash*. From Iran comes *Torshi-ye hafte-bijar*, a mixture of herbs, leeks, and spinach in a salted vinegar flavored with chili peppers, peppercorns, oregano, and garlic.

A popular savory preserve in Israel is *Zehug*, a hot relish made with fresh chili peppers, garlic, coriander seeds, and ground cumin. It originated in Yemen where it was served with beef casserole dishes on the Sabbath. Another Jewish relish, this time originating in eastern Europe, is *Chrane* (page 121), a mixture of horseradish and beets that is served with corned beef.

There are also many Middle Eastern fruit pickles. Lemons in oil, whole dried peaches and apricots, cherries on the stem, and whole grapes are favorites. Pickled orange peels and dates are often minced and then mixed with tamarind and sumac to make a version of uncooked chutney.

India, too, has a cuisine which values contrasting accompaniments, and probably no other country in the world makes as good use of so many mixtures of spices as can be found there. It is, of course, the home of chutneys–cooked, "keeping," and fresh chutneys.

Some cooked chutneys are made in a similar way to traditional Western chutneys, in which fruit and spices are simmered together for an hour or more. For some chutneys, ingredients such as mango or pumpkin are puréed raw and then cooked with the spices and vinegar for a short time only before being either bottled and stored for a long period or placed in the refrigerator for about a week only. The ingredients and preparation method determine the keeping time. Some keeping chutneys are not cooked at all. One Kashmiri chutney, for example, is made of brown sugar and vinegar mixed with large quantities of minced green ginger, garlic, mustard seed, and hot chili peppers, plus saffron and cayenne pepper. These are all mixed together, bottled, and left for a month before opening, resulting in a very spicy, pungent mixture, similar in texture to a well-cooked chutney, and with long keeping qualities.

Fresh chutneys are made just before serving using a wide range of fruits, vegetables, herbs, spices, and often yogurt. In the West, they probably would be regarded as relishes. Those with a yogurt base are sometimes called sambals or raitas. Some ingredients in fresh chutneys are puréed and some finely chopped, and there is always a good flavoring of herbs and spices. Some fresh chutneys are not hot at all and are eaten to tone down the spiciness of a curry. Others have a certain amount of heat which is very often derived from fresh ingredients such as green or red chili peppers or gingerroot. This gives a fresh taste to complement rich dishes of meat or vegetables.

Indian pickles are very spicy, with a certain degree of heat, and range from sweet to sour. Garlic, limes, cauliflower, and eggplants are common ingredients and the preparation often involves long marination in spices and salt. For some pickles, no other ingredients are added; some are covered in oil and a few in brine.

Many pickles and keeping chutneys can be bought already prepared in India, but the very nature of the fresh chutneys means that they are always especially prepared for every meal, using ingredients that are in season and readily available. Consequently, every family has its own unique recipes which are passed down from one generation to the next.

Across India's border into China, very few pickles are made in the home although a wide range of vegetables are pickled commercially. Although the Chinese enjoy eating pickles, there are very few available recipes. Two are included in this book, a simplified version of pickled spring greens (page 57) which comes from Kweichow, and a mixture of winter vegetables in brine (page 121), sometimes called *pow tsai*, which is probably the one most often made in Chinese homes. Other pickles enjoyed by the Chinese are Szechuan hot pickle, made from cabbage or kohlrabi, and snow pickle, made from mustard greens. These two are usually bought in cans. There is also a winter pickle of salted cabbage which can be bought in jars. Further east, in Japan, pickles are served with nearly every meal and, because their preparation is so simple, most are made in the home when needed.

Just one of the many varieties of Indian mango chutney that have been available over the years. Mango chutney has been popular in the West since the seventeenth century and the mango fruit has given its name to other imitation pickles and chutneys.

Cabbages and long winter radishes, or mooli, being stored on the window ledge of a house in Beijing.

A popular way of ending a meal is to serve a small portion of plain rice accompanied by tiny portions of pickle. Salt or soy sauce are often used as a single pickling ingredient. Sliced cabbage or white radish can, for example, be sprinkled with either or both ingredients and left for a few days until the juices have drained from the vegetable to form a natural pickling liquid. The Relish of Red and White Radishes (page 57) is made according to this method. Crisp and light, it is ideal for a quickly made pickle. Cucumber is treated in the same way as radishes. Pickles made like this will only keep for up to a week in the refrigerator. Another typical Japanese ingredient is *kombu*, a dried seaweed which is first stewed, then chopped and mixed with vinegar, soy sauce, sugar, rice wine, and sesame seeds to make a relish.

The simple pickling method used in Japan is also used in Korea, where the result is known as *kimchee*. Cabbage, white radish, cucumber, and turnip are favorite ingredients, and garlic cloves are pickled whole in a mixture of soy sauce, rice vinegar, sugar, and salt. These pickles are made at home and everyone has their own favorite ingredients.

From Indonesia and other parts of Southeast Asia come sambals or sambols. These are quickly made spicy relishes that are served with rice and hot curries. They are all made at home to accompany the favorite dishes of the household. Dried, hot chili peppers are ground with peanuts and tamarind paste; tomatoes are puréed in oil with cayenne pepper and lime juice; fresh chili peppers are pounded with garlic, peanuts, soy sauce, lime juice, tamarind, and sugar. In Ceylon a coconut sambal, made by mixing freshly grated coconut with chili powder, browned onions, lemon juice, and salt, is popular. *Seeni* sambal, also from Ceylon, is hot, rich, and made from browned onions, lemongrass, curry leaves, cinnamon, tamarind, fresh chili peppers, coconut milk, and dried shrimp. There are pickles, too, from the same areas, usually made by mixing the main ingredient, such as fresh pineapple or cooked eggplant, with vinegar, sugar, salt, and spices. These are eaten within a week of preparation.

And so to Europe, where, if anyone is asked what is the most pickled vegetable, the reply might well be the cucumber. There are

A pile of hot chilies in Thailand. Chilies are used in hot pickles and relishes in many parts of the world.

countless recipes for pickled cucumbers, mainly for the small ones which are sometimes called gherkins or (in France) *cornichons*, but also for the large variety, sliced or diced. In eastern Europe, dill pickles, small cucumbers in vinegar with sprigs of dill and peppercorns, are the favorite. In Scandinavia they are flavored with black-currant leaves and horseradish, and in France with thyme, tarragon, and bay. Baby cucumbers are not widely available fresh but tiny pickled gherkins bought in jars are popular with cold meats.

Cabbage is the only vegetable ingredient of German sauerkraut, a fermented pickle which takes several weeks to perfect. It is available commercially in cans and jars but many cooks still prefer to make their own. In Britain, plain red cabbage has been a popular candidate for pickling for more than a hundred years. Its rich color and crunchy texture make it an excellent accompaniment to cold meats. Also popular in Britain are pickled beets and pickled pearl onions, made with a simple brine of spiced vinegar. With bread and cheese, pickled onions make a "ploughman's lunch," and they are always sold alongside fish fried in batter.

Cauliflower usually appears in mixed pickles in Europe, particularly Italy and France, and it is an essential ingredient in Piccalilli (page 99). Teamed with broccoli, it makes a light, delicate springtime pickle.

SOUTHERN EUROPE

Peppers, tomatoes, and eggplants are the sun-kissed ingredients of southern Europe. They are often preserved in olive oil flavored with garlic, tomato paste, and warm spices such as paprika. Olives are pickled in brine both commercially and in the home. Green olives are picked when under-ripe, whereas black ones have become fully ripe on the tree. Garlic slivers, coriander seeds, and sprigs of herbs such as thyme or tarragon are all used to flavor olives.

The Europeans also specialize in making sweet pickles with seasonal fruits. In Italy, mixtures of fruits such as melon, grapes, and cherries are made into a mustard pickle. Pears, quinces, plums, apricots, and peaches are put into vinegar sweetened with sugar or honey. Cherries are pickled whole on the stem and even clementines and other small, sweet citrus

Fresh limes and lemons are used to make delicious, zesty pickles and relishes in India.

fruits can be pickled whole, complete with their skins. Fruit pickles are generally served with cold meats.

Very special to Britain, because of her historical relationship with India, are chutneys. Not the quickly prepared, fresh chutneys, but mixtures of fruits and vegetables, nearly always including onions, simmered for a great length of time with vinegar, sugar, dried fruits, and spices to the consistency of jam. Tomatoes, rhubarb, apples, and English marrows, similar to zucchini but larger, are other popular chutney ingredients.

There are very few relishes as such in Europe. Possibly the closest thing is Britain's mint sauce, which is served with roast lamb. It consists simply of chopped mint mixed with vinegar and a little sugar, and is similar to the fresh herb chutneys of India.

From Europe, as we have seen, pickles and chutneys traveled to the United States. Cucumbers with dill rapidly became popular as did a form of Piccalilli which came to be called "bread and butter pickles." Cherries, green peppers, mushrooms, olives, peaches, and prune plums soon found their way into the pickle jar, and it was not long before new ingredients were discovered and utilized, such as blueberries, watermelon rind, and corn. Chutneys also found their way to America via England directly from India through the spice trade.

AMERICAN RELISHES

The relish–the quickly prepared sweet-sharp mixture of vegetables which so often accompanies barbecued foods–has proved to be truly American. Corn relish, pepper relish, and tomato relish have become *de rigueur* whenever burgers or steaks are cooked, whether outdoors or in. They accompany sausages, cold meats, and vegetarian foods and they have traveled back to Europe in their new guise to become just as popular there.

American relishes were also influenced by the Mexican salsas, mixtures of chopped tomatoes, onions, and sweet or hot peppers that are used to top a *tostada* or *enchillado*. One such Mexican relish is the "Pico de Gallo" (rooster's beak), made with tomatoes, green onions, radishes, cilantro leaves, chili peppers, and lime juice. The recipe for pickled red onion slices (page 100) is based on a Mexican one which is served with chicken and seafood.

It is not far from South America to the Caribbean, where mangoes, papayas, and other exotic fruits are plentiful. Mangoes, in particular, are made into chutney, influenced by the Indian chutneys brought by the colonials of the eighteenth and nineteenth centuries. Mangoes are used when they are hard and under-ripe. They are simmered with golden raisins, cashew nuts, gingerroot, garlic, hot red chili peppers, brown sugar and malt vinegar in St. Kitts, and with tamarind and allspice in Jamaica. Quickly made relishes of puréed or finely chopped ripe mangoes and pawpaws mixed with lime juice and chili peppers also come from the Caribbean.

Wherever you go in the world, you will find a pickle, a chutney, or a relish to complement your meal and to tantalize your taste buds. All have been made using fresh, local produce and all show the character of the eating habits of the local people.

Corn and onion, waiting to be made into corn relish, which is popular throughout the United States.

INTRODUCTION

The basics

≈

Everything that you need

to make pickles, chutneys, and relishes

can be found in your local stores and

around your own kitchen.

Choose whatever fruits and vegetables

are in season and combine them with salt,

sugar, and vinegar, using nothing more

complicated by way of equipment than

a noncorrosive saucepan.

≈

INGREDIENTS

~

*GOOD-QUALITY VEGETABLES, FRESH AND DRIED FRUIT, AND HERBS ARE THE BASIC
INGREDIENTS FOR ALL PICKLES, CHUTNEYS, AND RELISHES. THEY ARE COMBINED WITH
VINEGAR, SALT, SUGAR, AND SPICES IN VARYING PROPORTIONS AND IN A VARIETY OF WAYS
TO ACHIEVE THE DESIRED END RESULT.*

FRESH FRUIT AND VEGETABLES

Although pickles and chutneys are an
excellent way to make use of seasonal
produce, they should never be regarded as
a way of salvaging aging or slightly below-
par ingredients. Fresh fruit and vegetables
should always be of the best possible quality
and any moldy or diseased fruit should be
discarded.

For pickling, vegetables must be young,
crisp, firm, and without any blemishes, and
they need to be prepared as soon as possible
after buying or harvesting so that their
crispness will be maintained. Fruit for pickling
should be only just ripe, so that it will remain
firm and retain its shape, even if simmered in
the pickling liquid.

The same rules apply to vegetables when
making chutneys, although tomatoes should be
ripe rather than hard and under-ripe, and
fruits, such as apricots or peaches, are better if
they are ripe and beginning to soften. Lower-
grade fruits can be used for chutneys since
they are cooked to a purée. You can use, for
example, small pears or irregular-shaped
apples, provided they are sound, without fear
of the end result being spoiled.

Young, crisp vegetables, fruit in excellent
condition, and sprigs of freshly picked herbs
are the essential ingredients for relishes. They
are made in a variety of ways, some being
slightly cooked and others being constructed
from completely raw ingredients.

DRIED FRUITS

Dried fruits are often included in chutneys
to add flavor and texture, as well as to replace
some of the sugar. Larger dried fruits, such as
apricots and dates, are usually chopped or
minced and smaller ones, such as raisins and
golden raisins, are used whole. Buy seedless
fruits of the best quality.

Whole dried fruits are also pickled and
added to relishes. Raisins and golden raisins
can be put into vegetable pickles, and in the
Middle East whole dried peaches and apricots
are pickled on their own.

VINEGAR

As a preservative, vinegar works by
penetrating and replacing the natural liquids
in food, inhibiting the growth of
microorganisms which would cause the
food to spoil or "go off."

Vinegar is a sharp-tasting liquid consisting
of dilute acetic acid produced as a result of the
fermentation of carbohydrates into alcohol,
followed by oxidation. The source of
carbohydrates for the original fermentation
may be fruit sugars, as used to produce wine or
cider vinegars, or rice, as in rice vinegar.

Whichever vinegar you choose to use, must
have a minimum acetic acid content of 5
percent. Bottled vinegars meet this
requirement. Until recently, many country

*A mixture of button
and oyster mushrooms
(far left). These, as all
vegetables should be for
pickling, are in perfect
condition.*

*Dried fruits are often
added to chutneys for
both sweetness and
flavor. There is a wide
variety to choose from.*

PURNELL'S PURE MALT VINEGAR

TRADE MARK

Brewery, Bristol, England. PLAIN & SPICED.

A 1920s advertisement for pure malt vinegar. Malt vinegar has a robust flavor and dark color. It is still popular for using in British pickles.

stores sold a product known as "raw or country" vinegar, which was excellent for salad dressings but did not come up to strength as a pickling acid. If your local store still stocks this, keep it for table use only.

Distilled vinegar, or white vinegar, produces a clear, smoother-flavored liquid. Distilled vinegar enhances the color of pickled vegetables and can help to maintain a lighter color when making certain chutneys.

Distilled vinegar can be bought already spiced for pickling. Although it can be a great time saver, its use can mean a loss of control over the final flavor of the pickle.

Wine vinegars are made from fresh wines. White-wine vinegar is usually slightly yellow or brown in color, rather like a pale white wine, and has a fine, subtle flavor. It is excellent for pickling delicately-flavored ingredients, such as mushrooms or asparagus. It can also be used in chutneys and relishes. Red-wine vinegar is red to rosé in color, depending on the brand, and more richly flavored than white-wine vinegar. It is useful

for pickling red ingredients such as red cabbage, beets, or red onions, or when making chutneys or relishes with red fruits such as plums or red currants.

Cider vinegar is produced from apples. It is darker in color than white-wine vinegar and has a distinctive cidery flavor. It is good for apple chutneys and relishes.

SALT

As part of the pickling process and when making some relishes, vegetables are salted–either sprinkled with salt or immersed in brine (a salted water solution). This draws water out of the vegetables which can then be replaced by vinegar. Salting also slightly toughens the vegetables, which helps to retain their crisp texture and improves the keeping qualities of a pickle.

Any noniodized salt is suitable for pickling. Avoid iodized table salt which may darken the colors of some fruits and vegetables. Most cooking salts are noniodized. So, too, are kosher salts, which are particularly suitable for this use but may be expensive. Salt sold in blocks is ideal. To separate the grains of this type of salt, rub a block on a grater or rub two blocks together.

Sugar

Sugar acts as both a flavorer and a preservative. It is an indispensable ingredient in chutneys. Vegetables and fruits can be pickled in a sweetened vinegar syrup. And some relishes call for the addition of a little sugar.

The type of sugar used very much affects the end result. As granulated sugar forms a colorless syrup, it is often used for pickles requiring a clear visual effect. It is also useful for light-colored chutneys. However, as long cooking of any type of sugar will produce a dark color, for a light-colored chutney it is wise to add the sugar toward the end of the cooking time.

Brown sugars contribute color and flavor, and generally the very dark, soft sugars, have the richest taste. Brown sugars are often used in chutneys and relishes. Demerara sugar, available from many health-food stores if your local supermarket doesn't stock it, produces a light golden-colored syrup and can be used for pickling.

Alternative sweeteners

Honey, molasses, and corn syrup can all replace some of the sugar content in chutneys and relishes. They will always add color and flavor. Honey makes a delicious pickling syrup for whole fruits such as apricots, cherries, and plums. Use the same weight as you would sugar. Dried fruits can also be used as a sweetener in chutneys, replacing some of the sugar content.

Spices

Most pickles, chutneys and relishes are flavored with spices.

For pickles, whole spices are used to flavor the vinegar. They can be either used loose or tied up in a small piece of cheesecloth to allow easy removal. A cheesecloth bag is the best method for making a sweetened vinegar syrup, for instance, where the fruits are generally simmered in the syrup along with the spices. Whole spices, such as dried chili peppers, cloves, or cinnamon sticks, are often put into

the pickle jars with the vegetables where they will continue imparting their flavor to the pickle for as long as it is kept.

In chutneys, which cook down to thick purées, spices are generally used ground. Recently bought ground spices give the best flavor; any that are older than six months should not be used.

Fresh gingerroot, chili peppers, and garlic are all considered as spices. Fresh ginger can be bought in the piece, peeled, thinly sliced, and in the same way as whole spices for flavoring vinegar. Chili peppers can be cored and seeded and then cut in half for flavoring vinegar or finely chopped for including in chutneys. Whole garlic cloves will flavor pickling vinegar and can be put into the jars with the vegetables. For chutneys, garlic is either crushed or finely chopped.

A selection of fresh ingredients, waiting to be pickled.

EQUIPMENT

~

MOST OF THE EQUIPMENT THAT YOU NEED TO MAKE PICKLES, CHUTNEYS,
AND RELISHES CAN BE FOUND IN ANY WELL-STOCKED KITCHEN.

CHOPPING AND GRINDING

Chopping boards and good, sharp vegetable knives are essential. For chutney ingredients, which have to be chopped into very small pieces, a food processor is ideal; it will save considerable time when preparing a large quantity of ingredients. Dried fruits do not chop easily in a food processor but they can be ground, along with other ingredients such as onions, using either a hand or an electric grinder.

SALTING AND MARINATING

Salting, soaking in vinegar, and marinating are normal processes in making pickles, chutneys, and relishes. Because the acid in salt and vinegars reacts with certain metals and can permeate absorptive materials, large bowls made of nonreactive and nonabsorptive materials are essential. Dissolved metals can taint or even poison the food and although a surface that becomes permeated with vinegar or brine will not damage food in any way, the bowl may not be suitable for any other purpose afterward. Strengthened glass, such as Pyrex, is the most suitable material. Plastic bowls may be used provided the surface is nonabsorptive. Glazed earthenware is not suitable because the salt or vinegar may damage the glaze.

To cover brined or marinating ingredients use plastic wrap.

For stirring the salting or marinating ingredients choose metal spoons which will not react or corrode. Stainless steel implements are the best.

COOKING

Special preserving pans or saucepans are ideal. Although expensive to buy, they will last a lifetime if properly cared for. If possible choose ones made of stainless steel or good-quality aluminum.

If ordinary saucepans are used, they should be made from a nonreactive material, such as stainless steel, aluminum, or enamel. Those with a high-quality nonstick finish are also suitable. Make sure that the coatings of enamel or nonstick pans are not chipped. Iron, brass, and copper pans are not suitable; their metals will react with vinegar, tainting the food and even, as in the case of copper, making it slightly poisonous.

Saucepans should be big enough to accommodate all the ingredients to about two–thirds full. Chutneys and vinegar syrups are very sticky and are difficult to clean off a stove if they boil over the edge of a saucepan that is too small.

Large stainless steel or wooden spoons are ideal for stirring ingredients while cooking. If you prefer using wooden spoons, keep special ones for making vinegar-based preserves as the vinegar permeates them and may taint other foods that you subsequently prepare with them.

A large, perforated spoon, preferably stainless steel, is necessary when making pickles that have to be removed from a liquid before being put into jars. A stainless steel ladle will also be useful.

Any straining, for example of spiced vinegar, should be done through a heatproof nylon strainer.

CANNING

An adequate supply of jars is, of course, essential. The most convenient size of jar is one that holds $1^1/2$ cups, generally referred to as a 1-pound jar since it holds by weight 1 pound of jam, marmalade, or honey.

Specific canning jars, made from tempered glass, with either spring-clip or screw tops, are excellent for all pickles, chutneys, and relishes. It is crucial not to allow any metal to come into contact with vinegar-based preserves because the metal will corrode and affect the flavor. Even when using plastic-coated tops, it is a good idea to place a disk of waxed paper in the lid as well. Chutneys can be covered with

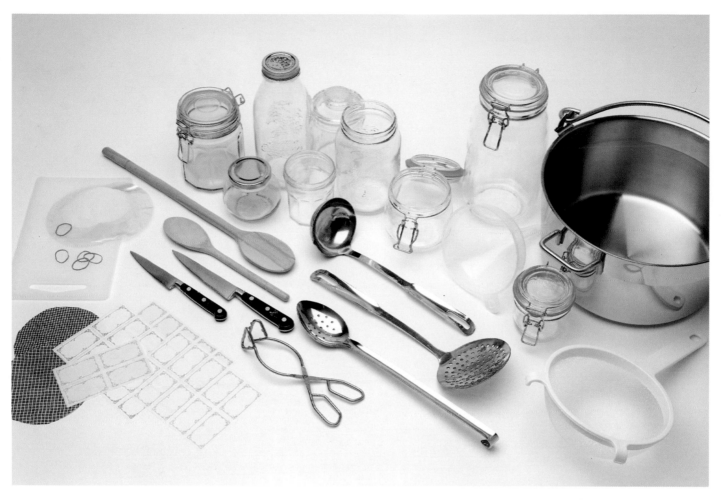

waxed paper disks before the tops are put on. Press these down well, making sure that no air bubbles are trapped underneath.

Simple jelly-pot covers–waxed-paper disks and an outer covering of plastic wrap or transparent cellulose–can be used for chutneys but are only completely effective if the chutney is stored in a dry, cool, well-ventilated place for no longer than six months. After this time, the vinegar may start to evaporate and the chutney will dry out.

All jars should be thoroughly cleaned and sterilized before use. To do this, wash and dry them, then lay them on their sides in a very low oven (200°F) and leave them for about 15 minutes. Before embarking on the final stage of pickle or chutney making, sterilize sufficient jars ready for filling; this will save last minute panics. Use the jars straight from the oven if the recipe calls for warm or hot jars but allow them to cool, without leaving them for too long, if the recipe calls for cold ones.

Transfer pickles, chutneys, or relishes to jars using a stainless-steel ladle. A stainless-steel or plastic, wide-mouth funnel to fit into the tops of most canning jars, is useful.

Sticky-backed labels to write the type of pickle or chutney and the date it was made, are essential. Plain ones are quite adequate for home use, but decorative ones add a special touch to any produce earmarked as gifts.

A noncorrosive pan, sharp knives, wooden spoons, perforated spoons, and ladles, jars, lids, and labels: all that is needed for successful pickle and chutney making.

Methods

≈

THE TECHNIQUES OF MAKING PICKLES AND PRESERVES

ARE VERY SIMPLE. TIME AND THE CHEMICAL REACTIONS

OF SALTS, OILS, AND VINEGARS, WILL DO MOST OF THE

WORK FOR YOU. STORAGE AND BOTTLING ARE THE KEYS

TO A FULL PANTRY ALL YEAR-ROUND.

≈

METHODS *for* MAKING
PICKLES, RELISHES, *and* CHUTNEYS

≈

WITHIN THEIR CATEGORIES, CHUTNEYS AND PICKLES USUALLY INVOLVE FAIRLY
STANDARD METHODS OF PREPARATION AS OUTLINED BELOW. RELISHES ARE A LITTLE
MORE DIVERSE IN THEIR METHODS OF PREPARATION. THESE ARE GUIDELINES ONLY,
AND INDIVIDUAL RECIPES SHOULD ALWAYS BE FOLLOWED.

VEGETABLE PICKLES

Pickles are usually made from raw vegetables that are packed into jars and covered with vinegar. The final flavor and texture of a pickle are determined by how they are treated and what other ingredients are added. The stages in making a vegetable pickle, plus a few variations and alternatives, are broadly as follows:

Initial preparation Some vegetables, such as onions or tomatoes, are peeled. Large vegetables are sliced or cut into even-size pieces. Small ones, such as pearl onions and small cucumbers, are left whole. Others, such as beets, may have to be cooked before pickling.

Brining To reduce the water content of vegetables, which would otherwise dilute the pickling liquid, the vegetables are often salted, either by dry-salting or brining. Individual recipes vary, and cooked or blanched vegetables may not need to be salted.

To dry-salt vegetables, they are first peeled and/or chopped to size. They are then layered in a bowl with salt, covered, and left for 12 to 24 hours.

To brine vegetables, they are completely immersed in a strong salt-and-water solution. Many recipes give precise proportions, but a good guide is $1^1/4$ cups of salt to $2\frac{1}{4}$ quarts

Shredding cabbage for pickling. A sharp knife will preserve the texture and shape of any vegetable. Cut your vegetables evenly so the pickle will look attractive in the jar.

water. A plate placed over the vegetables will hold them under the liquid. The bowl is then covered and the vegetables left for 12 to 24 hours.

After salting and brining, the vegetables are drained and usually rinsed with cold water and patted dry with paper towels.

Preparing vinegar Vinegar for pickling is usually flavoured with spices before it is poured over the vegetables. Ideally, preparation of the vinegar starts as soon as the salting process of the vegetables begins.

The desired quantity of vinegar is poured into a nonreactive saucepan and the required spices for the recipe are added. There are usually about 3 tablespoons of spices to 5 cups of vinegar. The vinegar is set over medium heat, and brought to a boil, then covered and simmered for 10 minutes. The pan is then removed from the heat and the vinegar left, still covered, until it is quite cool. Cooling takes about 2 hours, depending on the surrounding temperature. The vinegar can be strained as soon as it has cooled or left for as long as the vegetables are being salted, which results in a slightly more strongly spiced flavor. The spiced vinegar is strained through a nylon strainer into a pitcher for easy pouring over the pickles. The spices are then discarded.

To make a milder pickle, wine can be used to replace a proportion of the vinegar.

Preparing oil Oil can be used instead of vinegar for pickling. To flavor oil, whole flavorings, for example coriander seeds, herb sprigs, or garlic cloves, are added to it. It is then covered and left in a warm place for up to 12 hours.

Bottling When the vegetables are ready they are packed into sterilized jars; warm ones if the vinegar is hot, cold if the vinegar is cold.

To flavor the pickle after it is bottled, dried chili peppers, slices of ginger, herb sprigs, whole spices, or peeled garlic cloves can be pushed into the jars with the vegetables.

The vinegar is then poured over the vegetables to completely cover them. Any air bubbles must be dispelled by shaking or tapping the jar. If the vinegar is cold, the jars are sealed immediately. If it is hot, it should be left to cool completely before the jars are covered to prevent condensation forming, which would dilute the vinegar.

The jars are then labeled with the date

and type of pickle.

Storing Pickles are stored in a cool, dry place. They need to be kept for at least one week before opening to let the flavors fully penetrate the vegetables. Most vegetable pickles maintain their crispness for up to four months.

FRUIT PICKLES

Fruit is usually pickled in a syrup made from vinegar and sugar or honey.

Initial preparation Small fruits, such as apricots, cherries, or plums, are usually left whole. Pricking them in several places with a fork enables the vinegar syrup to penetrate more easily. The fruits are then packed into warm, sterilized jars.

Larger fruits, such as pears or peaches, are peeled. Fruits with a core (pears or quinces, for example), are quartered and the core cut away. Pitted fruits (peaches or nectarines, for example) are halved and the pit removed. The halves are either left intact or sliced.

Preparing the syrup and bottling The vinegar and sugar are stirred together into a nonreactive saucepan over low heat until the sugar dissolves. Whole spices to flavor the syrup are added at this point. They can be either loose or tied up in a small piece of cheesecloth for easy removal. The syrup is

Removing seeds from a honeydew melon. After this, cut the melon into wedges and cut the rind from each wedge, before evenly dicing the flesh.

boiled to release the flavors of the spices into it.

If the syrup is to cover whole fruits, it is boiled until it thickens and then is poured over the fruits. For pickling sliced fruits, the syrup is boiled briefly, the heat lowered, and the prepared fruits added and simmered slowly until they are cooked through but still firm. They are lifted out using a perforated spoon and packed into warm, sterilized jars. The syrup is then boiled until it thickens and is poured over the fruits.

In each case, the spices from the syrup may be either put into the jars with the fruits or removed. Additional spices, such as whole cloves, dried chili peppers, or pieces of cinnamon stick, can also be put into the jars at this stage.

The pickle is then left to cool completely before being covered and sealed. The jars are labeled with the date and type of pickle.

Storing Fruit pickles are kept for at least one week before being opened to let the flavors have time to penetrate the fruit. Most fruit pickles will keep for up to a year if stored in a cool, dry place.

CHUTNEYS

Chutneys are usually made with a mixture of fruits and vegetables.

Initial preparation All fruits and vegetables are finely chopped or ground. After being checked over, and peeled, they can be chopped by hand or in a food processor. A grinder is useful for tougher ingredients like dates or figs.

Dried fruits may be softened by soaking them in vinegar for up to 12 hours in advance, before the preparation of the fresh ingredients takes place.

Some recipes call for vegetables to be salted or brined in a similar way to pickle ingredients (page 36).

Cooking In simple chutney recipes, all the ingredients are usually put together in a saucepan or preserving pan, brought to a boil over medium heat and slowly simmered to form a thick purée with the consistency of jam. But some recipes do vary slightly.

Sugar produces a darker color when cooked for a long time. If a pale-colored chutney is required, white sugar is added after the rest of the ingredients have cooked down.

In some recipes, all or half of the vinegar is reserved until halfway through the cooking time.

At the beginning of the cooking time, a chutney will need to be stirred only about every ten minutes. However, toward the end of the cooking time, as the chutney becomes thicker, it will need frequent stirring to prevent it sticking to the bottom of the pan. The time that chutneys take to thicken varies from one to three hours. When they are thick, and bubbling, and a spoon dragged through the center leaves an impression that lasts for a few seconds, they are ready. The chutney is removed from the heat at this point and left until it has stopped bubbling.

Bottling As soon as the chutney has stopped bubbling, it is ladled into warm, sterilized jars. Between each ladleful the chutney is pushed down so any pockets of air are dislodged. Any drips or stickiness should be wiped off the jar or rim with a clean, damp cloth. The chutney is covered and sealed immediately. The jars are labeled with the type of chutney and the date.

Storing Chutneys improve and mellow with keeping so they should be left for at least one month, preferably longer, before being opened. Many chutneys will keep, unopened, for up to two years and maybe longer if stored in a cool, dark, dry cupboard. After this time, the level of chutney in the jar may begin to shrink as the vinegar evaporates and the contents dry out.

RELISHES

There are many different ways of making a relish. Some are a mixture of fresh ingredients, mixed together to be served immediately. Others are made in a way that is something of a cross between pickle and chutney procedures, as described below.

Initial preparation Vegetables and fruits for relishes are usually finely chopped and often lightly dry-salted or brined (page 36).

Cooking All the ingredients are put into a preserving pan or saucepan and cooked for 5 to 45 minutes. Some relishes are thickened by adding a mixture of flour or cornstarch and vinegar to the pan. After thickening, the relish is cooked for 2 to 5 minutes longer.

Bottling Cooked relishes for keeping are put into warm, sterilized jars and sealed immediately. They are labeled with the date and type of relish.

Storing Bottled relishes will keep for up to six months if stored in a cool, dry place.

PEACHES:—

Peaches make a delicious chutney, very similar to mango. They can also be sliced and put into a sweet, spiced vinegar.

RECIPES

RECIPES

Spring

≈

Bring a breath of fresh spring air

into your pantry by making savory

preserves with both homegrown

and imported fruits.

Use your imagination and find

vegetables such as leeks, spring greens,

and dried beans that you may have never

thought to preserve before.

≈

SPRING

~

IN SPRING, THE AIR IS CLEAR AND FRESH, NEW LIFE BURSTS OUT OF THE GROUND AND YOU HAVE SWEPT AWAY ALL THE COBWEBS IN THE HOUSE. NOW IT IS TIME FOR SOMETHING NEW IN THE PANTRY, SOME BRAND NEW SAVORY PRESERVES FOR SPRING. BUT WHAT PRODUCE IS THERE TO CHOOSE FROM?

Cucumbers, once only a summer vegetable, are now grown throughout the year and are excellent in the spring. Since early times, there have probably been more recipes for pickled cucumber than for any other vegetable.

Traditionally, springtime was still a very lean time of year, perhaps even the most precarious as the old saying makes clear: "March will tell, April will try but May will prove whether you live or die." What it meant was that with winter stores running low, there was really very little fresh produce to be had. The next season's crops were in the ground, but still only a few inches high. We hardly notice this today, now that food is jetted all over the world and cheats the seasons, but if you were to look at the vegetable garden in spring, what would you find?

Definitely leeks. Why else were they chosen as one of the emblems for St. David's Day, March 1 (the other Welsh national emblem is a daffodil)? Leeks withstand all the bad weather that winter can throw at them and actually grow in girth throughout the colder months without becoming tougher. With their green tops standing up from the ground like flags, they are the cook's promise of spring. Like onions, leeks are an excellent antidote to the common cold and many country people believed that eating leeks daily at this time of year would keep you healthy for a year. Another old saying goes:

Eat leeks in lide [March] and ramsons [wild garlic] in May, And all the year after physicians may play.

If you grow leeks yourself, you will know just how much dirt clings to them when they are pulled up. Wash them well under running water both before trimming and cutting to length and after. There is nothing worse than a gritty leek, whether in a stew or a pickle. Even if you buy your leeks trimmed and washed, wash them again under cold running water after chopping to length, just in case. If you need to store leeks at all, wash them, leave them whole, and put them in a plastic bag in

the refrigerator for up to three days. If they are left unrefrigerated, they tend to dry up.

Unlike onions, leeks are best cooked before pickling so they become really succulent after being steeped in the vinegar. They make an excellent accompaniment to all cold meals and are particularly good with pasta (page 55).

Broccoli is another spring garden favorite. As every plant seems to bear heads at the same time, to be able to turn them into a pickle is a great advantage. Most home gardeners grow what is known as "sprouting broccoli," which produces an abundance of small heads on side shoots. This is occasionally available in the stores but, since it is also sold with a large number of edible leaves attached, it is rather a waste to buy it simply for the heads. Instead, choose the larger-headed broccoli known as calabrese, which is also available at this time of year, and cut it into small flowerets. Both types of broccoli will keep in a plastic bag in the refrigerator for up to three days.

Although cauliflower is available all year, it is particularly flavorsome in spring when the hardy, overwintered varieties are ready for harvest. The crisp stems and crumbly textured flowerets have made the vegetable a favorite pickling ingredient for several centuries. Elizabeth Raffald's *Experienced English Housekeeper*, written in 1782, includes two recipes, one of which requires the salted cauliflowers to be laid out in the sun "till they are quite dry like scraps of leather" before the vinegar is poured over them. In India cauliflower stems are pickled, and in the Middle East cauliflower is pickled with dill or radishes. In the West a favorite cauliflower pickle has long been Piccalilli. However, as the other vegetable ingredients are not generally

Spring is traditionally the time when an abundance of fruits become available, and the later months of the season are especially plentiful.

Rhubarb is a wonderful standby in the spring. It grows prolifically in country gardens and is readily available in food stores. It makes a delicious chutney, especially when combined with dried fruits.

of producing them out of their once accepted season. In the northern hemisphere, cucumbers are produced in greenhouses nearly all the year-round and are particularly abundant in mid- to late spring. Although the sweet, firm, outdoor-grown cucumbers are not available in spring, these are often hard to find anyway, so, for the purposes of this book, I am regarding glasshouse cucumbers as an important supplement to the supply of fresh foods in spring. Of course, you can wait until the summer to use the recipes if you wish.

There are almost more recipes for pickled cucumbers than for any other single vegetable. They come from every century and from a wide variety of countries. In eastern European countries they are pickled with dill, in India they are mixed with yogurt and fresh coconut to make a refreshing sambal, and in Korea they are stuffed with white radish, fresh ginger, and scallions to make a pickle called "kimchee."

The white radish, sometimes called mooli, can be made into pickles and relishes on its own or with other ingredients (page 56). In Japan, where it is known as daikon, it is made into a relish with soy sauce. Closer to home, small, round, red radishes, with a fresher, less-musty taste than the white, become available in midspring. Use them alone or in combination with the white radish to make an interesting mix of flavors (see page 57).

EARLY FRUITS

For spring chutney recipes, you will have to look to the available fruits. The earliest suitable fruit to arrive, often as early as February, is rhubarb. Never regarded as a luxury fruit, rhubarb is a wonderful country standby, a valuable ingredient for fruit fools, pies, and crumbles when there is not any other fresh fruit to be had, and so prolific that most people give it away by the pounds. When cooked, it reduces down to a thick, textured purée, which makes it an ideal chutney ingredient. In fact, the edible part of the plant being the stalk, rhubarb is actually a vegetable and the slight vegetable quality about its flavor makes it blend well with onions and spices. Because of its very sharp flavor, chutneys must include plenty of dried fruits and sugar. Raisins are its natural companion, contributing sweetness and a mellow flavor to rhubarb's sharp pungency.

available in the spring to go with it, this is properly a fall recipe.

Choose cauliflowers that have large, firm, very white heads. If you need to store them before turning them into a preserve, keep them in the salad drawer at the bottom of the refrigerator for up to three days.

Spring greens, those hardy, dark green cabbages with no heart, are another successfully overwintered vegetable. It is unusual to find them in pickles in the West, but one of the few Chinese pickle recipes calls for their use (page 57).

It is unlikely that any present-day cook would run out of fresh vegetables to make into pickles, but in the eighteenth and nineteenth centuries cooks had to rely on dried vegetables, particularly beans, to see them through lean times. Kidney beans, in particular, were a popular pickle ingredient, and today garbanzo beans feature in Middle Eastern recipes (page 53).

Today, not only do we have efficient means of transporting vegetables but we are capable

Fresh rhubarb should have a shiny, almost translucent quality and should be crisp and not floppy. It can be stored for up to three days in a plastic bag in the refrigerator but, like most ingredients, it is best used as soon after buying or picking as possible. Always discard the leaves as these are poisonous and trim away the end of the stalk. Otherwise, rhubarb only has to be chopped.

EARLY FLAVORS

When homegrown fruits are scarce, you can turn to more exotic ones. Melons, grown all over the world, are available all through the year, but you can really appreciate them in spring. There are many varieties, but the honeydew is the one you are most likely to find at this time of the year. It is usually pickled in a sweet-sharp solution of sweetened vinegar (page 58). Melon is best teamed with mild spices, such as cloves, cinnamon, and mace, and a dark brown sugar is the best sweetener. In chutneys, melon is often treated like mango and there are various eighteenth-century recipes for "Melon, to make like mangoes," using garlic and pepper, cinnamon, and mustard seeds.

But why use a substitute when you can use the real thing? The most prolific of fruits, mangoes grow all over the world and are available all through the year. In the 1670s, members of the East India Company found mangoes in India where they were eaten fresh as well as being processed into chutneys and pickles. As the fruits could not withstand long sea journeys, the Company began exporting jars of pickled mangoes to Britain, where they were either used as they were or turned into more elaborate chutneys with other ingredients. The name for the fruit very soon became synonymous with the pickle and many recipes were entitled "To make a Mango" and used either the original fruit or substitutes.

Mango chutney is very special. The flesh softens and stays intact and blends easily with sugar, spices, and vinegar without losing its original flavor. There are mango chutneys from India, from the Caribbean (page 48), and from South Africa, as well as from the country kitchens of Britain and the United States. There are also what are sometimes called "fresh chutneys," mango flesh mashed and mixed with yogurt and lime juice as an accompaniment to spicy foods (page 60).

Papayas are not as sweetly juicy as mangoes, but their flesh is soft and rich and, either ripe or unripe, makes a good relish (page 60).

As you can see, even an unpromising season can offer a choice of foods for preserves, from humble rhubarb to exotic mangoes. So clear out your winter pantry and make way for a new supply.

Melons of all types are available in spring. Use them like mangoes in chutney or put them into sweet, spiced vinegar.

CARIBBEAN MANGO CHUTNEY

Very dark in color, this is a rich, hot, and fruity chutney that still maintains the fresh quality of the mango. Leave it for two weeks before opening and, once opened, it will keep for up to one month. Unopened, it will keep for up to two years.

FILLS ABOUT FIVE 1-POUND JARS

6 under-ripe mangoes
1 tbsp salt
2 ounces dried tamarind
1⅓ cups raisins, soaked for 12 hours
3¾ cups white vinegar
3 tbsp peeled and grated fresh gingerroot
2 fresh red or green chili peppers, cored, seeded, and finely chopped
2 cloves garlic, crushed
1¾ cups packed unrefined brown sugar

Peel and dice the mangoes. Put them into a bowl, mix in the salt, and leave them for 2 hours. Do not drain them. Put the tamarind into a bowl, pour 6 tablespoons boiling water over, and leave it for 30 minutes. Rub it through a strainer.

Put the raisins into a preserving pan or nonreactive saucepan. Pour in the vinegar and add the mangoes, the tamarind pulp, ginger, chili peppers, garlic, and sugar. Bring to a boil and simmer for about 1 hour, or until the mixture is thick. The mangoes should be tender but still in recognizable pieces.

Spoon the hot chutney into warm, sterilized jars and seal immediately.

Rhubarb *and* Orange Chutney

~

This is a bitter-sweet chutney with a distinct orange flavor that goes well with cold meats. Leave it for one month before using and, once opened, eat it within one month. Unopened, it will keep for up to three years.

FILLS ABOUT FIVE 1-POUND JARS

4 oranges, scrubbed
3 pounds rhubarb, chopped
  into 1-inch pieces
4 onions (about 1 pound),
  finely chopped (12 cups)
2¾ cups raisins

3¾ cups white vinegar
3½ cups packed light brown
  sugar
1 tsp ground mace
1 tsp ground cinnamon
1 tsp ground allspice

Thinly pare away the orange part of the peel and cut it into small, thin strips. Cut away and discard the white pith. Finely chop the flesh, reserving as much juice as possible and discarding as many seeds as you can.

Put oranges and their peels into a preserving pan or nonreactive saucepan. Add all the remaining ingredients. Bring them to a boil and simmer for about 2½ hours, or until the mixture is thick and dark.

Spoon the hot chutney into warm, sterilized jars and seal immediately.

Indian Rhubarb Chutney

~

Keep this hot, sweet, and spicy chutney for three weeks before using and, once opened, eat it within a month. Unopened, it will keep for up to two years.

FILLS ABOUT THREE 1-POUND JARS

3¾ cups white vinegar
2½ cups granulated sugar
3 pounds rhubarb, chopped
  into 1-inch pieces
10 cloves garlic, crushed
1 tsp cayenne pepper

2 tsp ground ginger
1 tbsp mustard powder
½ nutmeg, freshly grated
⅓ cup slivered blanched
  almonds

Pour the vinegar into a preserving pan or nonreactive saucepan. Add the sugar and set over low heat. Stir until the sugar dissolves. Add the rhubarb and cook slowly for 20 minutes, or until it has reduced to a purée.

Add all the remaining ingredients to the saucepan. Simmer gently, stirring occasionally, for about 2 hours, or until the chutney is thick and dark.

Spoon the hot chutney into warm, sterilized jars and seal immediately.

LEMON *and* GRAPEFRUIT CHUTNEY

The rich, dark brown of this unusual bittersweet chutney is flecked with mustard seeds and lighter pieces of citrus fruit. Leave the chutney for one month before using and, once opened, eat it within one month. Unopened, it will keep for up to two years.

FILLS ABOUT FIVE 1-POUND JARS

8 lemons	1⅓ cups golden raisins
2 grapefruit	3½ cups Demerara sugar
8 onions (about 6 cups),	2 tbsp mustard seeds
finely chopped	3¾ cups white-wine vinegar
2 tbsp salt	

Scrub the lemons and grapefruit and finely chop them, flesh and skin together, removing as many seeds as possible. Layer the citrus fruit and onions in a bowl with the salt. Cover and leave for 24 hours.

Put the citrus fruit and onions directly into a preserving pan or nonreactive saucepan, without draining them. Add all the remaining ingredients and mix well. Bring them slowly to a boil and simmer for 2 hours, or until the chutney is thick and dark.

Spoon the hot chutney into warm, sterilized jars and seal immediately.

Pickled Cucumbers

≈

Slightly salty and flavored with herbs, these crisp cucumber slices should be left for two weeks before using. Once opened, they must be eaten within a week. Unopened, they will keep for up to three months.

FILLS ABOUT FIVE 1-POUND JARS

4 large or 8 small cucumbers	*2 tsp coriander seeds*
7½ tbsp salt, plus 1 tbsp	*2 tsp black peppercorns*
6 tbsp chopped fresh dill or fennel	*3¾ cups white-wine vinegar*
2 tsp dill or fennel seeds	

Wipe and thinly slice the cucumbers, without peeling them. In a large bowl, dissolve the 7½ tbsp salt in 5 cups water. Add the cucumber and leave for 2 hours.

Pour the vinegar into a nonreactive saucepan with the remaining 1 tablespoon of salt. Bring to a boil, then remove from the heat and leave to cool.

Drain the cucumber slices in a colander and rinse them well under cold water. Layer them with the chopped fresh dill or fennel and the seeds and peppercorns in cold, sterilized jars. Pour in the vinegar and seal immediately.

Cauliflower *and* Broccoli Pickle

≈

Flowerets of cauliflower and broccoli make crunchy pickles, in this case, hot and spicy. Leave the pickle for at least three days before using and, once opened, it should be eaten within one week. Unopened, it will keep for up to three months.

FILLS ABOUT THREE 1-POUND JARS

3¾ cups white-wine vinegar	*1 piece fresh gingerroot, bruised*
2 tsp coriander seeds	*1 small firm cauliflower*
2 tsp cumin seeds	*2 large firm heads broccoli, or calabrese (about 1½ pounds)*
2 dried red chili peppers	

Pour the vinegar into a nonreactive saucepan. Add the coriander and cumin seeds, the chili peppers, and the gingerroot and bring to a boil. Cover and simmer for 10 minutes. Remove the pan from the heat. Leave the vinegar to cool completely, then strain it.

Cut the cauliflower and broccoli into small flowerets. Bring a pan of water to a boil. Put in the cauliflower and broccoli and blanch them for 1 minute. Drain them in a colander and run cold water through them. Leave them to cool.

Pack the cauliflower and broccoli into cold, sterilized jars and pour the vinegar over them. Seal immediately.

Hot Spiced Garbanzo Beans

An interesting addition to the range of spring preserves in the pantry, this hot, tomato-flavored pickle is Middle Eastern in origin and ridiculously easy to make. Serve it as a garnish to salad dishes. Do not use for at least one week. Once opened, the garbanzo beans should be eaten within a few days. Unopened, they will keep for up to two months.

FILLS ABOUT TWO 1-POUND JARS

2 x 15-ounce cans garbanzo beans
2 tbsp tomato paste
2 cloves garlic, crushed
2 tsp ground paprika
½ tsp cayenne pepper
⅔ cup olive oil
2 cups white-wine vinegar

Drain the garbanzo beans and pack them into cold, sterilized jars.

Put the tomato paste, crushed garlic, paprika, and cayenne pepper into a bowl and gradually work in the olive oil, 1 tablespoon at a time, to make a smooth paste.

Gradually beat in the vinegar. You can use a hand mixer or, alternatively, put all the ingredients together in a food processor and work until smooth.

Pour the mixture over the garbanzo beans and seal immediately.

A PICKLE *of* LEEKS *and* PINE NUTS

≈

A winter vegetable that overlaps into spring, leeks make a succulent pickle mixed with pine nuts and flavored with sweet spices. Leave the pickle for at least one week before using and, once opened, eat within two weeks. Unopened, the pickle will keep for up to four months.

FILLS ABOUT FOUR-AND-A-HALF 1-POUND JARS

3¾ cups white-wine vinegar
1 cinnamon stick
2 tsp allspice berries
2 blades mace
2 chips nutmeg (the small slivers left over when a whole nut has been freshly grated)
8 large leeks (about 4 pounds total weight)
1 cup pine nuts

Pour the vinegar into a nonreactive saucepan and add the cinnamon, allspice berries, mace, and nutmeg. Bring them to a boil, cover, and simmer for 10 minutes. Remove the saucepan from the heat. Leave the vinegar to cool completely. Strain through a nonreactive strainer.

Wash the leeks well, cut them into 1-inch pieces and wash them again. Bring a pan of water to a boil. Put in the leeks and cook them for about 7 minutes, or until they are just tender. Drain and allow them to cool.

Pack the leeks into cold, sterilized jars, sprinkling pine nuts in between. Pour the cold vinegar over them and seal immediately.

*Mooli and Cucumber Raita and
Relish of Red and White Radishes*

MOOLI *and* CUCUMBER
RAITA

≈

In India, long white radishes are known as mooli. Mixed with cucumber and a gently spiced yogurt, they make a refreshing relish to accompany curry. The relish should be served as soon as possible after it is made as it will not keep.

MAKES ABOUT 1¾ CUPS

*1 small white radish or mooli
(about 7 ounces)*
½ large cucumber
6 tbsp plain yogurt
1 tsp ground turmeric

1 tsp ground coriander
¼ tsp cayenne pepper
*2 tbsp golden raisins, finely
chopped*

Finely grate the white radish and finely chop the cucumber. Mix them together in a bowl.

Stir in the yogurt, turmeric, coriander, pepper, and golden raisins. Mix well and serve.

RELISH *of* RED *and* WHITE RADISHES

~

Radishes grow fast and abundantly in spring, and this crisp, light relish, good with curries and rice dishes, makes excellent use of them. The relish is ready to eat as soon as it has been prepared but it can be safely kept in the refrigerator, covered, for up to one week.

MAKES ABOUT 1½ CUPS

1 small white radish or mooli (about 7 ounces)
20 round red radishes
4 scallions, chopped
2 cloves garlic, crushed
1 tsp salt
1 tsp granulated sugar
¼ tsp cayenne pepper

Cut the white radish into ½-inch cubes and thinly slice the red radishes. Put all the radishes into a bowl and mix in the onion, garlic, salt, sugar, and cayenne pepper.

Transfer the mixture to a jar and cover with a piece of thin cotton material secured with an elastic band. Leave for 3 days at room temperature, occasionally pushing the radishes beneath the liquid that will collect.

Replace the cotton cover with a lid and place the relish in the refrigerator for 1 hour.

CHINESE PICKLED GREENS

~

Very light, salty, and hot, and with sweetness from the sherry, this pickle keeps the fresh flavor of the greens. Used sparingly, it is an excellent accompaniment for Chinese rice dishes. Although the preparation spans several days, the method itself is very easy. Leave the pickle for six weeks before using and, once opened, use it within two weeks. Unopened, it will keep for up to six months.

FILLS ABOUT TWO 1-POUND JARS

3 heads open green cabbage hearts or spring greens (about 2 pounds total weight)
6 cloves garlic
3 tbsp salt
2 tbsp dry sherry
1 tbsp chili powder
2 tsp granulated sugar
2 cups medium-dry sherry

Preheat the oven to 300°F.

Finely shred the greens and crush the garlic. Put them together into a casserole and cover. Place in the preheated oven and cook for 30 minutes. Remove the casserole and leave the vegetables to stand, covered, for 2 hours.

Sprinkle the vegetables with 1 tablespoon of the salt and the dry sherry. Cover again and leave to stand for 3 days at room temperature.

Mix in the remaining salt, the chili powder, and sugar. Pack the pickle into cold, sterilized jars. Pour in the medium-dry sherry and seal immediately.

MELON *and* MUSTARD PICKLE

Sweet melon cubes in a savory mustard sauce make this bright yellow pickle rather intriguing. Keep it for at least two days before using and, once opened, eat it within two weeks. Unopened, it will keep for up to six months.

FILLS ABOUT FIVE 1-POUND JARS

2 large honeydew melons
    (3 to 3½ pounds each)
3½ cups granulated sugar
2 tbsp mustard powder

1 tbsp ground turmeric
2 tsp ground ginger
2 tbsp cornstarch
1¼ cups white-
    wine vinegar

Cut the melon flesh from the rind and remove the seeds. Cut the flesh into ½-inch dice.

Put 1 cup water into a nonreactive saucepan with 2½ cups of the sugar. Set over low heat and stir until the sugar dissolves. Put in the melon pieces and simmer gently in the syrup for 10 minutes, or until they begin to soften and look translucent. Remove the pan from the heat and drain the melon, reserving the syrup.

In another bowl, mix together the mustard powder, turmeric, ginger, cornstarch, and half the vinegar. Put the remaining vinegar into a nonreactive saucepan and bring it to just below boiling point. Stir in the mustard mixture and continue stirring until it boils and thickens. Remove the pan from the heat and stir in 1¼ cups of the reserved syrup. Stir in the melon pieces.

Put the hot pickle into warm, sterilized jars and seal immediately.

SWEET-*and*-SOUR CUCUMBER
RELISH

≈

With a slight Chinese flavor, this light-textured, sweet-and-sour relish is good with poultry or lamb as well as vegetarian rice dishes. The relish is best served immediately after it is prepared but it will keep for up to three days in a covered container in the refrigerator.

MAKES ABOUT 1¾ CUPS

1 large cucumber	*⅔ cup white-wine vinegar*
1 onion	*1 tbsp soy sauce*
2 tsp cornstarch	*2 tbsp sunflower oil*
1 tsp ground ginger	*1 tbsp honey*

Wipe and very finely chop the cucumber, leaving the skin on. Very finely chop the onion.

Put the cornstarch into a small bowl with the ginger. Gradually mix in the vinegar and soy sauce.

Heat the oil in a saucepan on low heat. Put in the chopped onion and cook it for about 1½ minutes, or until it begins to look transparent. Stir in the cucumber, the cornstarch mixture, and the honey. Raise the heat to medium and bring the mixture to a boil, stirring constantly. Stir on the heat until the cucumber is in a thickened sauce, about 1 minute.

Remove the saucepan from the heat and turn the relish into a bowl to cool completely. Serve the relish as soon as it has cooled.

Mango Relish

Nothing can beat a good mango and this hot, spicy relish keeps all the fresh fruit flavor. Mangoes are often sold hard, but can be ripened at home, wrapped in newspaper and kept in a warm place such as the kitchen. Serve the relish on the day that it is made or store it in a covered container in the refrigerator for up to three days.

MAKES ABOUT 1 CUP

3 tbsp sunflower oil
2 green chili peppers, cored, seeded and finely chopped
2 cloves garlic, crushed
1 tsp ground cumin

1 tsp ground coriander
1 ripe mango, peeled and finely chopped
4 tbsp white-wine vinegar

Heat the oil in a skillet over low heat. Put in the chili peppers and garlic and stir on the heat for 1 minute. Add the cumin and coriander and continue stirring for 1 minute longer.

Add the mango and the vinegar to the pan and mix. Let the vinegar come to a boil and immediately remove the pan from the heat.

Put the relish into a bowl and leave to cool completely.

Papaya Relish

Light and fruity, this is a relish that goes well with cold meats and fish such as poached trout, salmon, or smoked mackerel. It is best eaten on the day that it is made.

MAKES ABOUT 1 CUP

1 ripe papaya
1 small onion
1 green chili pepper, or more to taste

½ lime, juice only
2 tbsp chopped fresh coriander

Halve and peel the papaya. Scoop out and discard the tiny black seeds from the center. Finely chop the flesh. Finely chop the onion. Core, seed and finely chop the chili pepper.

Put the chopped papaya, onion and chili together in a bowl, pour in the lime juice and mix well.

Thirty minutes before serving, place in the refrigerator to chill.

Summer

≈

SUMMER PRESERVES REFLECT THE

SEASON'S WARMTH AND ABUNDANCE.

FOR MANY MONTHS TO COME, YOUR JARS OF

SUMMER FRUITS AND VEGETABLES WILL

ADD COLOR TO YOUR PANTRY AND THE

FLAVOR OF THOSE SPECIAL MONTHS

OF THE YEAR TO YOUR TABLE.

≈

SUMMER

~

AS SUMMERTIME PROGRESSES AN INCREASING SUCCESSION OF DIFFERENT FRUITS AND VEGETABLES RIPEN. EACH FOLLOWS THE OTHER, PROVIDING A TIMETABLE FOR SUMMERTIME PRESERVING.

All this bounty comes in a wide variety of rich color. There are jewel-like red currants and black currants, soft, deep-red raspberries, black cherries, the blushing yellows of peaches and apricots, and the deep pink of watermelon flesh. There are bright green herbs for relishes and for adding in sprigs to pickle jars; green walnuts and the soft shades of asparagus and fava beans. Later on there are red tomatoes, green, red, and yellow sweet bell peppers, deep purple eggplants, and rich red plums. By the end of the season, your pantry can be lined with jars packed with brightly colored pickles, chutneys, and relishes; these jars will evoke the heady atmosphere of summer for many months to come.

Despite their wonderful appearance, soft fruits rarely figure prominently in recipes for pickles, chutneys, or relishes. Although raspberries can be used to flavor vinegar, vinegar does not seem to be used to flavor raspberries. However, raspberries can make a delicate pickle that is excellent with cold meats. If you would like to try this unusual accompaniment, follow the recipe given for blackberries (page 102), but reduce the final simmering time to five minutes instead of ten. For pickling, choose the plumpest raspberries you can find and make sure that they are not over-ripe; in fact, slightly under-ripe is preferable. Always use them on the day of purchase.

Black currants and red currants are not used for chutneys because their delicate flesh boils down to nothing during the long cooking time required, leaving only the seeds. They do, however, make excellent, fresh-tasting relishes. The short cooking time required softens the flesh without destroying its structure and their sharpness provides much of the necessary acidity without your having to add large quantities of vinegar. As with raspberries, always use black currants and red currants on the day of purchase and make sure that the fruit is sound. Remove the stems before cooking; this slightly tedious job is well worth the effort.

Cherries are an early summer delicacy. Their season is short and they all ripen together. In medieval times, before much preserving was done, "cherries on the rise" (on the twig) were hawked through the streets. In those days fresh fruit was scarce for much of the year so everyone ate as many cherries as they could so as not to waste them—sometimes with disastrous consequences! By the sixteenth century, however, cooks had learned how to preserve cherries, with the result that consumption of the fresh fruits could be more moderate and the residue could be enjoyed throughout the rest of the year.

Cherries, apricots, and raspberries can all be pickled whole in spiced vinegar. Choose them when they are firm and fresh.

A basketful of summer fruits painted in 1732. Plums, peaches, apricots, cherries, and green walnuts all make delightful savory preserves.

Young asparagus tips can be pickled in a mild vinegar, either alone or with mixtures of other summer vegetables.

Cherries are usually pickled whole, without pitting, and often with about 1 inch of their stem intact for easy handling when they are served. Pack them into clean jars and cover them with a vinegar spiced with mace, coriander, and black peppercorns. Alternatively, the vinegar can be sweetened and the cherries simmered in it for two minutes before bottling. Choose large, plump cherries for pickling and process them on the day of purchase.

Apricots arrived in the Western world at the time of the Crusades, and by the sixteenth century many European country houses had apricot trees growing against south-facing walls. By the end of the seventeenth century, apricot trees were already being grown next to farmhouses and settlements in America.

Like cherries, apricots had to be used up quickly, so they were often used for preserves, both sweet and savory. They were sometimes pickled whole in a sweet, spiced vinegar. In the eighteenth and nineteenth centuries, when chutneys and relishes became popular, apricots were found to be an ideal ingredient. Their flesh actually tastes better cooked than raw and they cook down to a soft, creamy textured purée that blends well with other ingredients. For pickling, choose apricots that are only just ripe, pale yellow with a soft pink blush. For chutneys, choose them riper and deeper colored if possible. Apricots will keep in a cool pantry for up to two days or in the refrigerator for up to four days but, like most fruits, they are best used on the day of purchase.

The name for apricot comes from the Portuguese "albricoque," which, in turn, derived via Arabic from Greek and Latin roots meaning "early ripening" because it ripened before the peach. Peaches, like apricots, were grown by sunny farmhouse walls and later in the large greenhouses that it became the fashion for every well-to-do European country house to have. Peaches were taken to South America by the Spanish in the sixteenth century and a hundred years later vast orchards were established in California. Also like apricots, peaches have long been a favorite pickle ingredient. A popular eighteenth-century recipe has them pickled in mustard-thickened vinegar, rather like a sweet Piccalilli. In chutneys, peaches behave very similarly to mangoes in that their flesh softens but remains in pieces or slices. Any recipe for mango chutney can be used for peaches. For pickling, choose peaches that are just ripe and for chutneys they should be ripe and juicy but not soft. The fruit will keep in a cool pantry for up to two days.

Watermelon, with its crisp, pink flesh resembling sweetened ice crystals, is harvested throughout the summer. In the seventeenth century watermelons were brought by African slaves to America where the peel soon became a common pickle ingredient. The flesh is too delicate for any sort of cooking or preserving process, but thrifty housewives soon discovered how not to waste all that peel. Soaked overnight in brine and simmered in a spiced, sweetened vinegar, it was transformed into a tasty pickle that would last through the winter.

At summer's end, come the plums. Many varieties are grown all over the world. Some are dessert varieties and others are better for cooking or preserving. Plums make a rich chutney—fruity flavored but slightly sharp (page 68)—and, with similar ingredients, they make a good, quickly prepared relish. Pickled plums have been popular in Europe since the seventeenth century. They are usually put into a sweetened vinegar, spiced with cloves, cinnamon, and allspice.

SUMMER SAVORIES

Along with the summer fruits are the summer vegetables. Most prized of all for savory preserving of all kinds must be the tomato (in reality a fruit, of course). Small ripe tomatoes can be pickled whole in either sweetened or unsweetened vinegar (page 76). Tomato relishes are made all over the world: the Mexican salsas, for example, often with chili peppers and sweet bell peppers; the tomato relish served so often with burgers and other fast food; the hot relishes of the Middle East, and the Indian tomato sambal.

When the tomato first arrived in the West from South America in the sixteenth century, it was looked on with great suspicion. Some regarded it as poisonous, some as an aphrodisiac (hence its old name "love apple"). It was not really until the early nineteenth century, when chutneys became popular, that the tomato came into its own, and if anyone has only ever made one type of chutney in their life, it is more than likely that it was based on tomatoes. As with cherries and apricots, if you grow your own tomatoes you tend either to have none at all or to have more than you can eat at any one time. Not surprisingly, at the end of the summer, the smell of tomato chutney wafts out from many a rural kitchen. For the other ingredients, most people use whatever they have in their pantry at the time. Some use golden raisins, others raisins; some white sugar, some brown, and some may even put in molasses. There are as many tomato chutney recipes as there are cooks who have made it.

Sweet bell peppers and green chili peppers are grown all over the world all through the year, but they are still essentially summer vegetables, their crisp textures and fresh flavors making ideal hot-weather food. It took a long time for peppers to be accepted in the West, yet, on looking at old recipe books, you will find that even Mrs. Beeton had a recipe for "Pickled Capsicums," in which the peppers are halved and seeded, brined and then put into a vinegar spiced with ground mace and nutmeg. Besides pickling, sweet bell peppers are used for quickly prepared relishes. From Bulgaria there is "Liutenitsa" which uses 1 pound each of sweet green bell peppers and chili peppers; from Tunisia a cucumber and pepper relish; and from Mexico, the various "salsas" in which peppers are

Common European Walnut
Juglans regia

mixed with tomatoes (page 72). Because peppers do not cook down to a purée they are never the main ingredient of a chutney. They are, however, often a complementary ingredient, such as in a tomato chutney, where they add both flavor and texture.

Although eggplants, or aubergines, like peppers, are now available all year, they are essentially a summer vegetable. They came originally from the Middle East, where they are still pickled in mixtures of spiced vinegar and oil. In Southeast Asia they are made into relishes and pickles, and in Japan they are served as a relish with a mustard and miso (fermented soybean) dressing.

The green vegetables of summer– asparagus, green beans, and fava beans–can all be put into light pickles, alone or together.

Unusual Delicacies

There are also some more unusual summer pickles. Pickled walnuts, picked when the nuts are green and with an undeveloped shell, soft enough to be pricked right through with a pin, have been popular in Britain since the sixteenth century (page 83). Unfortunately you cannot buy green walnuts; you have to be lucky enough to have access to a tree. Ash trees, however, grow wild, and you can pickle ash-keys (the seed pods) when they are immature, green and crisp in the middle of summer. Another summer pickle, perhaps the bonus of gardeners who leave their radishes in the ground so that they flower and seed, is pickled radish pods. The colors, textures, and flavors of summer pickles are virtually boundless.

Walnuts for pickling should be picked when they are green and tender enough that a needle can be easily pushed through the outer covering, shell, and kernel.

PLUM CHUTNEY

Plums make a sweet, fruity, dark purple chutney and adding apples gives a good, thick texture. Leave it for one month before using. Once opened, it should be eaten within 2 months. Unopened, it will keep for up to two years.

FILLS SIX TO SEVEN 1-POUND JARS

5 cups pitted and chopped plums (about 2 pounds whole)	2¼ cups packed Demerara sugar
2 large cooking apples, peeled, cored, and chopped (about 4 cups)	1 tsp ground ginger
	1 tsp ground allspice
	½ tsp ground cloves
4 onions, chopped	½ tsp grated nutmeg
3 cups raisins	¼ tsp cayenne pepper
	2½ cups white vinegar

Put all the ingredients into a preserving pan or nonreactive saucepan and bring slowly to a boil. Simmer for about 1 hour, or until the chutney is thick, stirring occasionally.

Spoon the hot chutney into warm, sterilized jars and seal immediately.

PEACH CHUTNEY

This fruity, dark chutney is interestingly spiced with curry flavors. Leave it for two weeks before using and, once opened, eat it within one month. Unopened, it will keep for up to one year.

FILLS ABOUT TWO 1-POUND JARS

8 peaches, ripe but firm	2 tsp ground coriander
2 tsp salt	½ cup packed Demerara sugar
2 tsp ground ginger	1¼ cups white vinegar
2 tsp ground cumin	

Halve, pit, and finely chop the peaches. Put them into a preserving pan or nonreactive saucepan with the rest of the ingredients. Bring slowly to a boil and simmer, stirring occasionally, for about 2 hours. The pieces of peach should stay intact but they will soften and become coated in a small amount of dark syrup.

Spoon the hot chutney into warm, sterilized jars and seal immediately.

Plum Chutney and Peach Chutney

NATURAL RED TOMATO
CHUTNEY

Take advantage of the summer's tomato glut to make a chutney with a natural, savory flavor and a bright orange-red color. This makes a wholesome replacement for bought ketchup. Keep it for two months before using and, once opened, eat it within one month. Unopened, it will keep for up to two years.

FILLS ABOUT FOUR 1-POUND JARS

4 pounds ripe tomatoes	*1 tbsp salt*
2½ cups finely chopped onions	*1 tsp ground cloves*
2 cups white vinegar	*1 tsp grated nutmeg*
1¼ cups granulated sugar	*1 tsp ground allspice*

Put the tomatoes into a large bowl. Pour boiling water over them and leave them for 1 minute. Drain them and peel them, then finely chop them.

Put the peeled tomatoes and onions into a preserving pan or nonreactive saucepan with ⅔ cup of the vinegar. Bring gently to a boil and simmer for about 30 minutes, or until the onions are soft.

Add all the remaining ingredients and simmer for 1½ hours longer, or until the chutney is thick.

Spoon the hot chutney into warm, sterilized jars and seal immediately.

EGGPLANTS
PICKLED *in* OIL

~

Slices of salted lemon lighten the flavor of this rich pickle. Buy unwaxed lemons; alternatively scrub them well. Leave the pickle for at least three weeks before using. Once opened, it should be eaten within two weeks. Unopened, it will keep for up to four months.

FILLS ABOUT TWO 1-POUND JARS

2 lemons
1½ tbsp salt
3 large eggplants (about
   12 ounces each)

2 tsp ground paprika
approximately 1 cup
   olive oil

Wipe and thinly slice the lemons. Put them into a bowl and sprinkle them with 1 tablespoon of the salt. Leave them for 1 hour, then drain them.

Cut the eggplants into ½-inch thick slices. If their circumference is large, cut them in half crosswise. Bring a pan of water to a boil, add the eggplants, and simmer them for 7 minutes, or until they are soft but firm. Drain them and pat them dry with paper towels.

Put the cooked eggplant slices into a bowl. Mix together the remaining salt and the paprika and add to the eggplants. Toss to make sure that the slices are evenly coated.

Pack the eggplants into cold, sterilized jars, putting in 2 lemon slices between each layer. Pour in the olive oil to cover them completely. Seal immediately.

Tomato *and* Green Pepper Relish

≈

Good with burgers, sausages, and all barbecued food, this rich tomato relish can be served immediately or it can be kept in a covered container in the refrigerator for up to two weeks.

MAKES ABOUT 2½ POUNDS

8 tomatoes
4 tbsp olive oil
1 onion, finely chopped
1 clove garlic, finely chopped
1 green bell pepper, cored,
*   seeded, and diced*

1 small green chili pepper,
*   cored, seeded, and diced,*
*   optional*
2 tbsp dark unrefined sugar
4 tbsp white vinegar

Put the tomatoes into a large bowl. Pour boiling water over them and leave them for 1 minute. Drain and peel them.

Heat the oil in a saucepan over low heat. Put in the onion and garlic and cook them for 2 minutes. Stir in the bell and chili peppers and cook for 2 minutes longer, stirring occasionally, until they begin to soften.

Turn the heat up to medium and add the tomatoes. Stir to heat through. Stir in the sugar. When it dissolves, add the vinegar and bring it to a boil. Remove the pan from the heat and leave the relish to cool completely.

Peach Relish

≈

Good with curries, rice dishes, or plain meats, this fruity relish can also be made with one teaspoon of hot curry powder in place of the paprika and cayenne. It can be eaten on the day that it is made, or it can be kept in a covered container in the refrigerator for up to five days.

MAKES ABOUT 1 CUP

2 ripe peaches
4 tbsp olive or sunflower oil
1 small onion, finely chopped

1 tsp ground paprika
¼ tsp cayenne pepper
4 tbsp white-wine vinegar

Put the peaches into a bowl and pour hot water over them. Leave them for 1 to 2 minutes depending on ripeness. If the peel will come off easily after 1 minute, they are ready to peel. Drain them and then peel and finely chop them.

Heat the oil in a saucepan over low heat. Put in the onion and cook for about 3 minutes until soft. Increase the heat to high and stir in the peaches. Sprinkle in the paprika and cayenne, then pour in the vinegar. Let the vinegar boil, then remove the pan from the heat. Leave the relish to cool completely.

RED CURRANT
RELISH

≈

Good with poultry, game, and lamb, this fruity, sharp-sweet relish can be served immediately or it can be kept in the refrigerator in a covered container for up to one week.

MAKES ABOUT ⅔ CUP

4 tbsp olive or sunflower oil	*2 tsp honey*
1 small onion, finely chopped	*8 ounces red currants, stringed*
4 juniper berries	*4 tbsp red-wine vinegar*
4 allspice berries	

Heat the oil in a saucepan over low heat. Put in the onion and cook it for about 3 minutes to soften it.

Crush the juniper and allspice berries together using a mortar and pestle. Mix the crushed spices with the honey, then add the red currants and onion. Increase the heat to high. Pour in the vinegar, stir, and bring to a boil. Remove the pan from the heat and leave the relish to cool.

Green Peppers *layered with* Eggplant Relish *in* Spiced Oil

This is a rich pickle of contrasting flavors. Leave it for two weeks before using and, once opened, eat it within one week. Unopened, the pickle will keep for up to one year.

FILLS ABOUT SIX 1-POUND JARS

8 small green bell peppers	*1 tbsp coriander seeds*
2 eggplants	*1 tbsp cumin seeds*
2 onions	*⅔ cup white-wine*
6 tbsp salt	*vinegar*
2½ cups olive oil	

Very finely chop the eggplants and thinly slice the onions. Put each separately in a bowl. Sprinkle the eggplants with 4 tablespoons of the salt and the onions with 2 tablespoons.

Cover them and leave for 12 hours. At the same time, put the olive oil into a bottle or bowl and add the coriander and cumin seeds. Leave it for 12 hours.

Rinse and drain the eggplants. Bring a saucepan of water to a boil. Put in the eggplants and simmer them for 5 minutes or until they are soft but still intact. Drain and leave them to cool. Rinse the onions with cold water and drain them well. Mix together the eggplants and onions.

Core and seed the peppers, then cut them into thin, lengthwise strips.

Layer the peppers with the eggplant and onion mixture in cold, sterilized jars. Strain the oil and pour it into the jars, taking care that all the spaces in the jars become filled. Seal immediately.

HOT-SPICED RED TOMATO CHUTNEY

≈

Darker than the Natural Red Tomato Chutney (page 70), this chutney has a hot, spiced flavor. Keep it for two months before using and, once opened, eat it within one month. Unopened, the chutney will keep for up to two years.

FILLS ABOUT TWO 1-POUND JARS

4 pounds ripe tomatoes
3 cups finely chopped onions
2 cloves garlic, crushed
2 cups white vinegar

1¼ cups granulated sugar
1 tbsp ground paprika
1 tsp cayenne pepper
2 tsp mustard seeds

Put the tomatoes into a large bowl. Pour boiling water over them and leave them for 1 minute. Drain them and peel them, then finely chop them.

Put the peeled tomatoes into a preserving pan or nonreactive saucepan with the onions, garlic, and ⅔ cup of the vinegar. Bring to a boil and simmer for about 30 minutes or until the onions are soft.

Add the remaining ingredients and simmer for 1½ hours longer, or until the chutney is thick.

Spoon the hot chutney into warm, sterilized jars and seal immediately.

SWEET PICKLED TOMATOES

≈

The slices of tomato in this sweet, mildly spiced pickle are tender and have a natural, red color. Leave the pickle for one week before using. Once opened, eat it within two weeks. Unopened, it will keep for up to four months.

FILLS ABOUT TWO 1-POUND JARS

4 pounds tomatoes,
   ripe but not soft
4 tbsp salt
2½ cups white-wine vinegar
2½ cups packed Demerara
   sugar

2 cloves garlic
2 blades mace
1 cinnamon stick
2 tsp allspice berries

Wipe the tomatoes and cut them crosswise into ¼-inch thick slices. Put them into a bowl, layering them with the salt. Cover and leave them for 24 hours. Drain them.

Put the vinegar into a nonreactive saucepan with the sugar. Peel the garlic cloves and tie them in a piece of cheesecloth with the mace, cinnamon stick, and allspice berries. Put the cheesecloth bag into the pan. Bring the vinegar to a boil over medium heat, stirring until the sugar dissolves.

Add in the tomatoes, lower the heat, and bring the vinegar slowly back to a boil. Simmer for 1 minute longer.

Carefully lift out the tomatoes using a pancake turner and pack them into warm, sterilized jars.

Bring the vinegar back to a boil and boil for about 15 minutes, or until it is thick. Leave it to cool slightly, then pour it over the tomatoes. Leave the pickle to cool before sealing.

A Mixed Pickle *of* Summer
Vegetables

FILLS ABOUT SEVEN 1-POUND JARS

*1 small cauliflower, cut into
    small flowerets*

*1½ cups green beans topped,
    tailed and cut into 1-inch
    pieces*

8 small carrots, thinly sliced

*2 yellow bell peppers, cored,
    seeded, and cut into 1-inch
    strips*

*2 red bell peppers, cored,
    seeded, and cut into
    1-inch strips*

*4 red or green chili peppers,
    cored, seeded, and very
    thinly sliced*

*16 scallions, cut into 1-inch
    pieces*

*6 to 7 garlic cloves (one per
    jar), peeled*

*6 to 7 fresh dill sprigs (one per
    jar) or fennel sprigs*

3¾ cups white-wine vinegar

⅓ cup plus 2 tbsp salt

Leave this light, crunchy, colorful pickle for at least six weeks before using. Once opened, it will keep for up to two weeks. Unopened, it will keep for up to four months.

In a large bowl, mix the cauliflower, green beans, carrots, bell peppers, chili peppers, and scallions together. Then pack them into cold, sterilized jars, distributing the smaller quantities such as the chili peppers and scallions equally. Put 1 garlic clove and 1 dill sprig into each jar.

Pour the vinegar into a nonreactive saucepan, add the salt and 3¾ cups water. Set the saucepan over high heat and bring the contents to a boil. Remove from the heat and leave to cool slightly. Pour the vinegar solution over the vegetables and seal immediately.

Cilantro *and* Mint Relish

≈

With a beautiful, bright green color and a fresh, hot flavor, this relish is good with all Indian curries. It is best eaten the day it is made, but it may be kept in the refrigerator in a covered container for up to three days.

MAKES ABOUT 1¾ CUPS

1 cup chopped fresh cilantro
1 green chili pepper, seeded and chopped
2 tbsp freshly squeezed lemon juice
1 ounce fresh mint
2 tsp grated fresh gingerroot
½ tsp salt
6 tbsp plain yogurt

Put 1 tablespoon of the cilantro into a food processor with the chili pepper, lemon juice, and 2 tablespoons water and blend to a purée. Add half the remaining cilantro and blend again. Add the mint, ginger, and salt and blend to a smooth, green purée. Add the remaining cilantro and blend again.

Put the yogurt into a bowl. Mix in the contents of the blender. Place in the refrigerator and chill for 30 minutes before serving.

Creole Relish

≈

With a fresh, clean, hot tomato flavor, this relish will keep in a covered container in the refrigerator for up to one week.

MAKES ABOUT 1¾ POUNDS

6 tomatoes (about 1 pound)
½ lime, juice only
1 tsp salt
¼ tsp cayenne pepper
1 onion, finely chopped
1 stick celery, finely chopped
4 pimiento-stuffed olives, finely chopped

Put the tomatoes into a large bowl. Pour boiling water over them and leave them for 1 minute. Drain and peel them.

Put the peeled tomatoes into a food processor with the lime juice, salt, and cayenne pepper. Work them to a purée.

Put the onion, celery, and olives into a bowl. Mix in the tomato purée. Cover, place in the refrigerator. Chill for 30 minutes before serving.

Sweet Spiced Apricots

Whole apricots are used in this mildly spiced honey pickle. Serve it with cold meats and pâtés. Leave the pickle for one month before using. Once opened, it will keep for one month. Unopened, it will keep for up to nine months.

FILLS ABOUT SIX 1-POUND JARS

3 pounds apricots
24 cloves or 4 per jar
1-inch piece cinnamon
*   stick per jar*
*   (approximately 6)*

3¾ cups white-wine vinegar
1 pound honey

Prick the apricots all over with a fork. Pack them into cold, sterilized jars. Put 4 cloves and a piece of cinnamon stick into each jar.

Put the white-wine vinegar and honey into a nonreactive saucepan and stir them over low heat until the honey dissolves. Raise the heat to medium and bring the syrup to a boil. Boil it for 5 minutes or until it is beginning to thicken.

Remove the saucepan from the heat and leave the syrup to cool slightly, then pour it over the apricots. Leave the pickle until it is cold before sealing.

Pickled
Walnuts

~

If you have access to the fruit of a walnut tree, you are indeed fortunate and will be able to make this mild, onion-flavored pickle of soft walnuts. The walnuts have to be green, that is when you can easily push a pin through both the outer coating and the young shell. The process of salting the walnuts is spread over nine days, but is well worth the effort. Leave the walnuts for at least two weeks before using and, once opened, eat them within one month. Unopened, they will keep for up to two years.

FILLS ABOUT TWO 1-POUND JARS

3 pounds green walnuts with skins
3 pounds and six ounces salt
4 shallots
6 cloves garlic or 2 per jar
2 tbsp preserved grated horseradish
2 quarts white vinegar

Wash the walnuts. Put them into a large bowl and cover them with boiling water. Leave them until the water has cooled completely. Dissolve ½ cup of the salt in 2 quarts cold water.

Wearing rubber gloves so you don't stain your hands, take the walnuts out of the water one by one and scrape off the thin outer skins, then drop each immediately into the brine. Leave them to soak for 24 hours.

Drain the walnuts. Put them into a bowl and pour boiling water over them. Leave them to cool. Make fresh brine with the same quantities as before and soak the walnuts in this for 24 hours longer. Repeat the process seven more times.

After the last soaking in brine, drain the walnuts. Put them into a bowl and cover them with cold water. Leave them for 10 minutes and drain them again.

Thinly slice the shallots. Peel the garlic cloves and leave them whole.

Pack the walnuts into cold, sterilized jars, putting in pieces of shallot, two garlic cloves per jar, and a little of the horseradish.

Pour the vinegar into a nonreactive saucepan and bring it to a boil. Leave it to cool to lukewarm, then pour it over the walnuts. Seal immediately.

RECIPES

Fall

≈

In Fall, with so much fresh produce

available, pickling and preservation become

almost necessities.

Be like the squirrel and line your

pantry with rows of glowing pickles

and chutneys to take the end of summer

into the beginning of winter.

≈

FALL

≈

*FALL IS THE SEASON OF PLENTY, WHEN MORE FRUITS AND VEGETABLES ARE
READY FOR HARVESTING THAN AT ANY OTHER TIME OF THE YEAR. THE ABUNDANT
PRODUCE OF SUMMER'S END—JUICY TOMATOES, CRISP BELL PEPPERS, AND FRESH GREEN
BEANS—OVERLAPS WITH THOSE SPECIAL INGREDIENTS THAT MAKE THEIR BRIEF
APPEARANCE DURING THOSE FEW MONTHS LEADING UP TO THE END OF THE YEAR—
SQUAT PUMPKINS, GOLDEN QUINCES, NUTS, WILD MUSHROOMS AND, OF COURSE, GREEN
TOMATOES THAT WILL RUN OUT OF SUNSHINE BEFORE THEY ARE ABLE TO RIPEN.
THERE ARE ALSO THE ROBUST VEGETABLES THAT WILL SEE US RIGHT THROUGH THE
COLD OF WINTER—THE MANY KINDS OF ONIONS, THE CABBAGES,
THE FIRST CELERY, AND MAIN-CROP CARROTS.*

Apples are at their best in the fall months. Use them to make thick, sweet-sharp chutneys.

It is a rich time, indeed, when the activities of pickling and preserving, always a pleasure, almost become a necessity. It would be a pity to waste home-grown produce or neglect the store bargains going cheap, so you are tempted to stock up with rows of glowing pickles and chutneys to enjoy during the bleak season ahead.

Blackberries are suddenly everywhere–wild ones in the hedgerows and their cultivated brothers in the stores. Even the most timid of wild food gatherers must have been blackberry picking at some time in their life and experienced the double satisfaction of not only having made an excellent preserve, but of actually having gone out to gather the ingredients instead of finding them on a supermarket shelf. Although wild blackberries are not as uniformly fat and succulent as cultivated ones, they often have a finer flavor, and seasoned blackberry pickers usually have their favorite patch where they know the fruits grow large and sweet.

While there is plenty of advice on how to make blackberry jam, there are few written recipes for making savory preserves. The seeds render blackberries unsuitable for chutney, but they do make an excellent pickle that goes well with red meats and game (page 102). Blackberries should be used as soon as

possible after picking or buying. It is advisable to rinse both types of fruit in cold water before use, then drain them well.

Another fruit that you may find both wild and cultivated is the damson, like a small, dark purple plum with a soft blue bloom on its skin. In the United States, dark red Sierra plums, the beach plum, and the Chickasaw plum can be used instead. All of these fruit are small, with a bitter flavor when raw. Although there are no recipes for pickled damsons, they do make good relishes (page 90). Damsons will keep for up to four days in the refrigerator but are best used on the day of purchase or harvest. When preparing damsons for making a chutney, it is best to pit them first. This is slightly time-consuming but well worth the effort.

Apples and pears are now available all year-round, but, in the northern hemisphere at least, they are all harvested in the fall. This is when you can buy them straight from the tree instead of from the cold store. Modern methods of storage are wonderful but there is still nothing like freshly picked fruit. It has all of its crispness, its flavor, and its juiciness. Using fruit at this time of year ensures the best possible quality preserves.

The old way of preserving apples for the winter was to cut them across into rings and hang these on sticks to be stored in the attic or

Apples and pears from the eighteenth century. The favorite way of using pears at the time was to pickle them whole in a sweet, spiced vinegar.

Apples	S.D.E.W.	6	Red Calvil.	S.D.E.	11	White Muscatell.	S.D.E.W.	16	Oxford Gold.n Grasan	S.D.E.W.	22	Bez: y D Hyver	S.D.E.W.	28	Rough St Germain.	S.D.E.W.
1	Windsor Pearm.n	SDE	7	Golden Pearmain	SDE	12	Warners lt Spanish		17	Lashasserie	DEW	23	Spanish boon	SDE	29	St Andren	DEW
2	Red Cour pendue	DE	8	Silver Pippin	SDE	13	Blue Goswell	EE	18	Rouslet D LaReine	DEE	24	Ambrett	DEE		The Maple	
3	White Calvil.	SDE		Grapes		14	White Madera		19	Amadott	DE	25	Angelica	DEW	A	leav'd Service	
4	Wheelers Russet.	SDE	9	Malmise.			Pears		20	Virgo luce	DEW	26	Golden Bell	SDE	B	Great Bulless	S
5	Broad'ee	SDE	10	Restling or Renish	s	15	Grasan.	DEE	21	Monsieur John.	SDE	27	Mashes gr.n butter	DEE	C	Yellow Haugh	SD

NOVEMBER 1732

Design'd by Pt Casteels.

From the Collection of Robt Furber Gardiner at Kensington 1732.

Engrav'd by Jam.s Smith.

Nearly every gardener who grows tomatoes has green ones left over in the fall. They can be pickled whole in a sweetened vinegar or used to make a pungent flavored chutney.

barn to dry. In the nineteenth century, when chutneys became popular, apples, especially the cooking varieties with their ability to cook down to a fluffy purée, were recognized as the ideal ingredient. There are even recipes of the time called "mango chutney" but which did not contain any mangoes at all, just apples, dried fruit, and spices. Although apples are not usually the main ingredient for a pickle, Mrs. Beeton included in her original book of 1861, a recipe for "An Excellent Pickle," which consisted of diced cooking apples, cucumber, and onions in a pickling liquid of soy sauce, sherry, and vinegar.

Because of their firmer texture, pears are often made into a pickle, usually with a liquid made from sugar and vinegar (page 96). They can be diced, sliced, quartered or even, if small, left whole, and put into jars with cloves or red chili peppers to add to the flavor and appearance. Ripe pears also make a good chutney.

The quince is available only in the fall and usually only direct from small producers or from your own garden. Golden yellow and shaped like a small, waisted pear, this unusual fruit has a rich, honeyed, pungent flavor. It can be pickled, like a pear, becoming a deep pinky-gold color when cooked in the liquid, or it can be chopped and added to apple chutneys, using fewer quinces than apples because of their stronger flavor. Quinces keep well in a cool, dry pantry for about two weeks.

All kinds of nuts arrive in the stores and markets in the fall and the shelled kernels can be included whole in sweet pickles or ground and mixed with herbs, onions, or garlic and yogurt to make sambals and relishes. The kernels of recently picked nuts have a fresh, crisp, and milky texture.

GREEN TOMATOES

The greenhouse and the sunny garden produce dozens of green tomatoes in the fall. In countries with a temperate climate, most gardeners are left with many late-formed tomatoes which will never ripen outside due to lack of strong sunshine. Most end up in pickles and chutneys. Once skinned, green tomatoes cook down to a fluffy purée similar to apple purée and so are an ideal ingredient for chutneys and relishes (see pages 93 and 99). Small tomatoes can be pickled whole, in a sweet-sharp syrup of sugar and vinegar, spiced with a few cloves.

English marrows, a type of fully grown zucchini, are another vegetable that grow all through the summer. But as they are so prolific it is rare for them to all end up as a savory vegetable. Their sheer abundance, as well as a natural aptitude, makes them a good preserving ingredient. It was discovered very early on that they made an excellent substitute for mangoes in a chutney and there are many recipes for what is called "Marrow Mangoes" (page 95). They have a light texture, but plenty of spices are needed to turn them into a robustly flavored chutney.

A relative of the marrow is the pumpkin. Brought to the United States by the Pilgrim Fathers, it quickly became a favorite vegetable. Its creamy-textured, golden flesh cooks down to a smooth purée, making it an ideal ingredient in chutneys (page 91). It can also be cubed to make a glowing gold pickle.

Corn is often used fresh for relishes. Frozen and canned corn is available all the year, but the firm texture of kernels which have been freshly cut from the cob is far superior.

Onions and shallots are harvested at the beginning of fall. Onions are indispensable to most chutneys, adding the essential savoriness to sweet fruits and sugar. Pickled pearl onions are popular and, together with cheese, make a delicious lunch. They can be salted in plain spiced vinegar or in a sweetened vinegar. Shallots can be treated in the same way. Sliced large onions make an unusual onion pickle, whether you use white fleshed or red fleshed varieties (page 95).

Garlic, also harvested in early fall, is often added in small quantities to chutneys and pickles as part of the flavoring, but it can also be the main ingredient, especially in relishes. For instance, mixed with some green chili peppers and cilantro and pounded together in a little olive oil or water, it makes a biting, refreshing relish which regularly accompanies dishes in India and is also known in Jewish cooking as *zehug*.

PLENTIFUL MUSHROOMS

Mushrooms are artificially grown and sold all year-round now, but many nostalgic country dwellers still think of them as fall treats. There is nothing quite like walking through orchards on a crisp, dewy morning and filling a basket with mushrooms. Few people are lucky enough to be able to do this today, so buy the commercially grown ones and allow their scent to conjure up for you pictures of misty lanes on fall mornings as you pickle them (page 93). There are dozens of old recipes for pickling mushrooms, the reason being that they were once so abundant in fall that it seemed as if you only had to walk past a spot and they would grow up behind your back.

INTERNATIONAL FLAVORS

Many fall vegetables can be put into mixed pickles: the crisp, mustard-coated combinations known as Piccalilli and based on an old Indian recipe (page 99); the green tomato and chili pepper pickles of Mexico; or the carrot, green bean, pepper, cucumber, or cauliflower pickles of the Middle East. Mixed pickles are an excellent way of using up small surpluses of a variety of vegetables. With this type of recipe you can often substitute one for another or vary the quantities according to what you have available.

An unusual pickle from Britain worth mentioning is pickled nasturtium seeds. The British once had a liking for capers, small, pickled buds

with a pungent flavor, which were mostly imported. In the sixteenth century it was discovered that the seeds of nasturtium flowers, if pickled as soon as the flowers had wilted, would make an excellent substitute. Nasturtium seeds pickled in vinegar have a pungent flavor similar to that of capers but with a slight peppery overtone. They are an easy pickle to make. Methods vary, but basically, after being dry-salted or soaked in brine, they are rinsed, drained, and dried, then packed into a jar, together with a few herbs such as tarragon or dill and peppercorns if desired, and covered with a white-wine vinegar; some people spice the vinegar first. As there is virtually no preparation and the quantities involved are small, nasturtium seeds are a good introduction to fall pickling.

Wild mushrooms, as well as the cultivated, can be pickled, but it is important to know whether they are safe to eat or not.

QUINCE *and* APPLE CHUTNEY

≈

The apples in this sweet, golden brown chutney cook down to a thick purée but the small, lighter colored pieces of quince remain more firm. Store the chutney for one month before using. Unopened, it will keep for up to two years.

FILLS SIX TO SEVEN 1-POUND JARS

8 quinces (about 1 pound)	*2 tsp ground mace*
4 large cooking apples (about 2 pounds)	*2 tsp ground cloves*
	2½ cups cider vinegar
12 onions (about 3 pounds)	*2¾ cups Demerara sugar*
3 cups golden raisins	

Peel, core, and finely chop the quinces and apples. Finely chop the onions.

Put the chopped quinces, apples, and onions into a preserving pan or nonreactive saucepan with the golden raisins, mace, cloves, and vinegar. Bring them slowly to a boil and simmer for 20 minutes, or until the apples are soft.

Stir in the sugar and continue to simmer, stirring occasionally, for 1½ hours, or until the mixture is soft and thick.

Spoon the chutney into warm, sterilized jars while it is still hot and seal immediately.

DAMSON *and* DATE CHUTNEY

≈

Rich, thick, and dark, this sweet chutney makes excellent use of tough-skinned damsons, small blue-black plums which are too tart to be eaten raw. The riper the damsons are, the easier they are to pit; run a sharp knife all around each one, pull the two halves apart and then ease out the pit. Keep the chutney for one month before using. Unopened, it will keep for up to two years.

FILLS ABOUT THREE 1-POUND JARS

3 pounds damsons, pitted	*1 tbsp mustard seeds*
2¼ cups finely chopped, pitted dried dates	*1 tsp ground allspice*
	2 cups red-wine vinegar
¾ cup dark unrefined sugar	

Put all the ingredients into a preserving pan or nonreactive saucepan. Bring slowly to a boil. Turn down the heat and simmer gently, uncovered, for about 1¼ hours, or until the mixture becomes very thick.

Spoon the chutney into warm, sterilized jars while it is still hot and seal immediately.

PUMPKIN CHUTNEY

Golden brown with a creamy texture, this is a good savory chutney. Leave it for at least two weeks before using. Unopened, it will keep for up to one year.

FILLS SIX TO SEVEN 1-POUND JARS

3 pounds pumpkin
*8 ripe tomatoes (about
    1 pound)*
4 onions (about 1 pound)
*2 large cooking apples (about
    1 pound)*
1⅓ cups golden raisins
*2½ cups light unrefined
    sugar*

2 tsp salt
*1 tsp freshly ground black
    pepper*
2 tsp ground ginger
1 tsp ground allspice
3 cups white vinegar

Cut the peel and seeds from the pumpkin and discard them. Finely chop the flesh. Bring a saucepan of water to a boil, add the pumpkin, and simmer for 10 minutes. Drain well and mash to a purée.

Peel the tomatoes. Cut a cross in the peel at the bottom of each and place them in a bowl. Cover them with boiling water, and leave for 10 to 30 seconds. Plunge them into cold water. Peel.

Cut each peeled tomato in half. Scoop out the seeds, rub them through a strainer and reserve the juice and flesh. Finely chop the flesh.

Finely chop the onions. Peel, core, and finely chop the apples.

Put the chopped onions, apples, and tomato flesh and juice into a preserving pan or nonreactive saucepan. Add all the remaining ingredients and bring slowly to a boil. Reduce the heat and simmer gently for 2 hours, or until the chutney is thick.

Spoon the chutney into warm, sterilized jars while it is still hot and seal immediately.

GREEN TOMATO CHUTNEY

~

Those who grow their own tomatoes are always on the look-out for a new recipe to use up unripened fruit before the frosts arrive. This is a light, fresh-tasting chutney with a good green color. Leave it for at least two weeks before using. Unopened, it will keep for up to one year.

FILLS ABOUT FOUR 1-POUND JARS

3 pounds green tomatoes
2 green bell peppers
3 onions (about 12 ounces)
3 cooking apples (about 1½ pounds)
1¼ cups granulated sugar

grated peel and juice of 1 lemon
1 tbsp salt
1 tsp freshly ground black pepper
1 tsp ground mace
1 tsp ground ginger

Put the tomatoes into a saucepan and cover them with water. Bring slowly to a boil and simmer them for 15 minutes. Using a slotted spoon, remove and peel one tomato at a time, keeping the unpeeled ones immersed. Cut the tomatoes in half and scoop out the seeds. Rub them through a strainer and reserve the flesh and juice. Finely chop the flesh.

Core, seed, and finely chop the bell peppers. Finely chop the onion. Peel, core, and finely chop the apples.

Put the tomato flesh and juice with the chopped peppers, onion, and apple into a preserving pan or nonreactive saucepan and add all the remaining ingredients. Bring them slowly to a boil and simmer for up to 2 hours, or until the mixture is thick.

Spoon the chutney into warm, sterilized jars while it is still hot and seal immediately.

MUSHROOMS PICKLED *in* WHITE WINE

~

Preserved in a light wine and vinegar pickle, these mildly spiced mushrooms retain all of their succulence. Leave the pickle for at least one week before using. It will keep for up to two months, but once a jar has been opened, the pickle should be eaten within a few days.

FILLS ABOUT SIX 1-POUND JARS

3¾ cups white-wine vinegar
2 dried red chili peppers
2 blades mace
1 small piece dried gingerroot, bruised
3 pounds button mushrooms

2 tbsp salt
about 1½ cups dry white wine, plus extra for topping up as necessary
sprigs of thyme, one for each jar, optional

First, prepare the spiced vinegar. Pour the vinegar into a nonreactive saucepan and add the chili peppers, mace, and ginger. Bring to a boil, lower the heat, and simmer, covered, for 10 minutes. Leave the vinegar to cool completely, then strain it.

Spread the mushrooms out on a flat dish. Sprinkle them with the salt and leave them for 30 minutes. Drain the mushrooms but do not rinse them.

Put the drained mushrooms into a wide-bottomed saucepan and set them over low heat. Cook them for about 3 minutes, turning them occasionally, until their juices begin to run. Increase the heat and cook, stirring, for 5 minutes, until they are cooked through and have produced their own juices.

Pour in the spiced vinegar and simmer the mushrooms in it for 10 minutes. Remove the saucepan from the heat. Let the mushrooms cool, then put them and the vinegar into a plastic container. Cover and leave for 24 hours.

Strain the mushrooms, reserving the vinegar, and pack them into warm, sterilized jars. Measure the vinegar (there should be about 1½ cups) and mix it with an equal quantity of dry white wine. Pour the liquid over the mushrooms. If there is insufficient liquid to cover them, distribute what there is evenly between the jars and then top up with more white wine.

Push one thyme sprig into each jar, if you like. Seal the jars.

Mushrooms Pickled in White Wine

SWEET SPICED ONION SLICES

~

Gently spiced with cloves, this is a sweet onion pickle. Small button mushrooms can be pickled in the same way: peel them and salt them whole, then proceed with the recipe as for sliced onions. Leave the pickle for one week before using. Unopened, it will keep for up to four months, but once opened, it should be eaten within one week.

FILLS ABOUT FIVE 1-POUND JARS

12 onions (about 3 pounds)	*2¼ cups granulated sugar*
2 tbsp salt	*1 tbsp cloves*
2½ cups white-wine vinegar	*12 dried red chili peppers*

Slice the onions very thinly into rings. Layer them in a bowl with the salt, cover, and leave for 12 hours. Rinse the onions with cold water and drain them well.

Put the vinegar, sugar, cloves, and chili peppers into a nonreactive saucepan and stir them over low heat until the sugar melts. Bring to a boil and simmer for 5 minutes.

Pack the onions into warm, sterilized jars. Pour the hot vinegar over them, ensuring the cloves and chilies are evenly distributed among the jars. Seal immediately.

MARROW CHUTNEY

~

Tasting like mangoes after a long simmering, as so many early marrow chutneys recipes were designed to do, this hot, spicy, and sweet brown chutney is good with curries. Leave for at least one week before using. Unopened, the chutney will keep for up to one year.

FILLS ABOUT FIVE 1-POUND JARS

1 large or 2 small English marrows (about 4 pounds)	*2 tbsp ground coriander*
6 onions (about 1½ pounds)	*1 tsp ground cumin*
2 pounds Demerara sugar	*1 tsp cayenne pepper*
grated peel and juice of 2 lemons	*2 tsp salt*
	4½ cups white-wine vinegar

Peel the marrow. Cut it into quarters and remove and discard the seeds and pith. Cut the flesh into ¼- x 1-inch pieces. Thinly slice the onions.

Put the chopped marrow and sliced onions into a preserving pan or nonreactive saucepan together with all the remaining ingredients. Bring slowly to a boil. Lower the heat and simmer, stirring occasionally, for about 3 hours, until the pieces of marrow are very tender and the juices reduce and thicken. The chutney will not look as thick as one that cooks to a purée, such as an apple chutney, but it will thicken as it cools.

Spoon the chutney into warm, sterilized jars while it is still hot and seal immediately.

PICKLED PEARS

Tender, mildly spiced slices of pear in a sharp-sweet pickle are an excellent way to make use of cheap and plentiful fruit in the fall. Keep the pickle for one week before using. Unopened, it will keep for up to six months. Once opened, it must be eaten within one week.

FILLS ABOUT FOUR 1-POUND JARS

1 stick cinnamon, broken
6 cloves
1 small piece dried gingerroot, bruised
2½ cups white-wine vinegar

3¾ cups granulated sugar
6 small pears (about 4 pounds)
dried chili peppers, one for each jar

Tie the cinnamon, cloves, and gingerroot in a small piece of cheesecloth.

Put the spice bag into a nonreactive saucepan with the vinegar and sugar. Set the saucepan over low heat and stir until the sugar dissolves. Bring the syrup to the boil and remove the saucepan from the heat.

Bring a saucepan of water to a boil. Meanwhile, peel and quarter the pears and cut out their cores. Put the pears into the boiling water and blanch them for 5 minutes. Drain them.

Bring the syrup to a boil again and add the pears. Turn the heat down and simmer for about 15 minutes, until they are tender but still firm and they appear translucent.

Using a slotted spoon, lift the pears out of the syrup and pack them into warm, sterilized jars. Put one dried chili pepper into each jar.

Remove the spice bag from the syrup and boil the syrup again for about 5 minutes, or until it is thick. Pour the hot syrup over the pears. Seal immediately.

PICCALILLI

~

Almost any combination of crunchy vegetables can be used to make this perennial mustard pickle, but the selection below works very well. Leave the pickle for one week before using. Unopened, it will keep for up to three months. Once opened, it should be eaten within two weeks.

FILLS ABOUT SIX 1-POUND JARS

1 large cucumber	*1 tbsp mustard seeds*
1 small English marrow or	*1 tsp black peppercorns*
6 zucchini (about	*4 dried red chili peppers*
1 pound)	*½ cup Demerara sugar*
1 large cauliflower (about	*2 tsp ground ginger*
2 pounds)	*1 tbsp ground turmeric*
4 onions (about 1 pound)	*1 tbsp mustard powder*
2 tbsp salt	*2 tsp all-purpose flour*
3¾ cups white vinegar	

Wipe but do not peel the cucumber. Cut it into ½-inch dice. Peel the marrow, cut it in half, and remove the seeds. Chop the flesh into ½-inch dice. If you have zucchini instead of marrow, wipe and thinly slice them. Chop the cauliflower into 4½-inch pieces. Chop the onions.

Put all the chopped vegetables into a large bowl and toss in the salt. Leave for 12 hours. Drain the vegetables in a colander, rinse them through with cold water, and drain them again.

Pour 2½ cups of the vinegar into a nonreactive saucepan and add the mustard seeds, peppercorns, and chili peppers. Bring to a boil and simmer, covered, for 10 minutes. Strain the vinegar and return it to the saucepan.

Put the ginger, turmeric, mustard powder, and flour into a small bowl and gradually mix in the unused vinegar. Stir the mixture into the hot vinegar in the saucepan. Bring the mixture to a boil and stir in the vegetables. Simmer for 10 minutes, stirring occasionally.

Leave the pickle to cool completely, then pack it into cold, sterilized jars. Seal the jars immediately.

Piccalilli

GREEN TOMATO *and* APPLE RELISH

~

The tomatoes and cooking apple in this hot, bittersweet relish provide all the necessary sharpness. The relish can be used on the day that it is made or it can be kept in a covered container in the refrigerator for up to two weeks.

MAKES ABOUT 2 CUPS

12 green tomatoes (about	*4 tbsp olive oil*
1 pound)	*¼ tsp ground allspice*
4 green chili peppers	*¼ tsp salt*
2 onions (about 8 ounces)	*2 tbsp light unrefined*
1 cooking apple (about	*sugar*
8 ounces)	

Put the tomatoes into simmering water and simmer them for 15 minutes. Remove the saucepan from the heat. Peel and finely chop the tomatoes, taking each one out of the saucepan when you are ready to peel it.

Core, seed, and finely chop the chili peppers. Finely chop the onions. Peel, core, and chop the apple.

Heat the oil in a saucepan over low heat. Put in the onion and cook for about 3 minutes until softened. Add the tomatoes, chili peppers, apple, allspice, salt, and sugar. Simmer them, covered, for 20 minutes, to make a thick, pureéd mixture.

Turn the relish into a bowl and leave it to cool.

RED ONION
RELISH

Based on a Mexican recipe, this mild, crisp, and light purple-red relish will add interest to casserole and rice dishes. It may be eaten the day after preparation but will keep for up to one month if bottled. Once opened, it must be stored, covered, in the refrigerator and eaten within one week.

FILLS ABOUT TWO 1-POUND JARS

*4 large red onions (about
    1 pound)*
1 tbsp salt
*1 tsp dried oregano or
    marjoram*

*1¼ cups white-wine
    vinegar*
juice of ½ lemon

Thinly slice the onions. Put them into a bowl and scatter them with the salt. Leave for 30 minutes.

Pour boiling water over the onions and drain them immediately. Leave them to cool.

When the onions are completely cool, pack them into cold, sterilized jars, adding a little of the oregano or marjoram to each jar.

In a bowl or measuring jug, mix together the white-wine vinegar and lemon juice with 6 tablespoons water. Pour over the onion slices. Seal the jars immediately.

CORN *and* CHILI RELISH

The corn kernels used to make this light, unthickened relish should either be freshly cut from the cob or frozen; canned kernels will not hold their shape to give the relish its textured structure. You can either use the relish immediately or you can bottle it for use within two months; once opened, it should be used within one week.

FILLS ABOUT ONE-AND-A-HALF 1-POUND JARS

2 green or red chili peppers	*½ tsp salt*
1 green bell pepper	*½ tsp mustard powder*
1 cup corn kernels	*2 cups white-wine*
2 tbsp sugar	*vinegar*

Core and seed the chili peppers and finely chop them. Core, seed, and finely chop the bell pepper. Put the chili and bell peppers into a nonreactive saucepan and add the corn kernels.

In a bowl, mix together the sugar, salt, and mustard powder. Gradually stir in the vinegar, then pour the mixture into the saucepan.

Set the pan over medium heat and bring the contents to a boil. Simmer, uncovered, for 15 minutes, or until the corn is just tender.

Leave the relish to cool completely and serve immediately, or store it in a covered container in the refrigerator for use within one week. Alternatively, spoon it, while still warm, into warm, sterilized jars and seal immediately.

PICKLED BLACKBERRIES

Blackberries make an eye-catching purple pickle with a rich, fruity flavor that is good with all kinds of cold meats. Leave the pickle for one week before using. Unopened, it will keep for up to one year.

FILLS ABOUT THREE 1-POUND JARS

2 tbsp allspice berries	*small piece dried gingerroot,*
4 cloves	*bruised*
1-inch piece cinnamon	*2 cups white vinegar*
stick	*3 pounds blackberries*
	1¾ cups Demerara sugar

Put the allspice berries, cloves, cinnamon, and ginger into a nonreactive saucepan and pour in the vinegar. Bring slowly to a boil, cover, and simmer for 10 minutes.

Strain the spiced vinegar into a bowl. Add the blackberries while it is still warm, cover, and leave for 12 hours.

Strain the blackberries, reserving the spiced vinegar. Pour the vinegar into a saucepan, add the sugar and bring to a boil. Add in the blackberries and simmer, uncovered, for 10 minutes, or until the blackberries are tender but still retain their shape.

Using a slotted spoon, lift out the blackberries and put them into warm, sterilized jars. Pour the spiced vinegar syrup over them and seal immediately.

Corn and Chili Relish

WALNUT *and* CILANTRO RELISH

≈

Based on an Indian recipe from Kashmir, this rich walnut relish is a good accompaniment for curry. It should be eaten as soon after preparation as possible.

MAKES ABOUT 1 CUP

1 cup shelled walnuts	¼ tsp cayenne pepper
6 tbsp chopped fresh cilantro	4 tbsp plain yogurt
juice of ½ lemon	

Put the walnuts into a food processor and finely chop them. Add all the remaining ingredients and work into a paste.

MUSHROOM RELISH

≈

This rich, delicately flavored relish can be served immediately it is prepared or stored in the refrigerator in a covered container for up to two weeks. It can also be bottled and kept, unopened, for up to one month.

FILLS ONE 1-POUND JAR

8 ounces open-cup mushrooms	6 tbsp red-wine vinegar
1 onion	4 tbsp chopped fresh parsley
1 clove garlic	½ tsp black peppercorns,
3 tbsp olive or sunflower oil	coarsely crushed

Very finely chop the mushrooms, preferably using a food processor. Finely chop the onion and garlic.

Heat the oil in a nonreactive saucepan over low heat. Put in the onion and garlic and cook for about 3 minutes to soften them.

Raise the heat to medium. Pour in the vinegar and bring it to a boil. Add the mushrooms, parsley, and peppercorns. Bring them to a boil, lower the heat, and simmer, uncovered, for 10 minutes, or until the mushrooms are cooked through.

Either let the relish cool and serve, or, while still hot, spoon it into a warm, sterilized jar and seal immediately.

Walnut and Cilantro Relish

RECIPES

Winter

≈

WINTER IS AN IDEAL TIME FOR MIXING

THE MUNDANE WITH EXOTIC, THE SAVORY WITH

THE SWEET, TO PRODUCE PICKLES AND CHUTNEYS

WITH RICH, WARM COLORS AND SPICY-HOT FLAVORS

TO CHEER UP THE LONG, DARK DAYS.

≈

WINTER

*WINTER DAYS MAY BE LONG AND DARK, BUT HAPPILY THE COLORS OF WINTER FOODS
ARE RICH AND WARM. FILL YOUR JARS WITH ORANGE CARROTS AND YELLOW RUTABAGAS,
PURPLE-RED CABBAGE, AND BEETS AND CRIMSON CRANBERRIES.*

Make your winter chutneys full flavored and spicy, with a touch of hotness to warm you through chilly days. Make pickles that are robust enough to contrast well with warming winter casseroles and stews, as well as being ideal complements to the roast meats and cold spreads of Thanksgiving and Christmas.

Ingredients at this time of year are full of contrasts. On the one hand there are roots and cabbages, and on the other all the special dried fruits and nuts which are brought to prominence for the period leading up to Christmas. There are plenty of fresh fruits, too, such as apples and pears which keep well in store, lemons, limes, and sweet and Seville oranges, plus big, juicy pineapples, black and white grapes, and bananas. Winter is an ideal time for mixing the mundane with the exotic, the acid with the sweet, to produce savory preserves for your own table and also for giving away as presents.

At one time, before fruit could be stored for long periods or transported across the world, most fresh fruits were used up by midwinter and all that was left were home dried apples

The best dried fruits can be bought in the winter. Used in chutneys to replace some of the sugar, they provide both flavor and sweetness.

and, if you could afford them, imported dried fruits. That is why most traditional Christmas foods have dried fruits as their main ingredient. Think of plum puddings and the large, rich fruit cakes.

Dried fruits are full of concentrated sweetness. For many years, when sugar was relatively more expensive than it is today, dried fruits took its place in a wide variety of recipes. Now, both dried fruits and sugar are readily available and can be used together to enhance the flavors and textures of wintertime preserves. Besides the usual currants, raisins, and golden raisins, look for the extra large seedless raisins, plump, whole apricots, moist figs and dates, shiny black prunes, halved pears, and whole or halved peaches.

Chopped candied peel can make an interesting bittersweet addition to chutneys so it is well worth buying some at the same time as your dried fruits. You can buy it in one piece, in which case it has greater preserving qualities, or, for greater convenience, chopped and in a light coating of sugar syrup.

The big advantage in buying dried fruits is that they keep well, so if you find varieties that are available only at this time of the year (peaches or pears for example), buy them now. Put them, still in their packages, into an airtight container and store them for up to four months in a cool cupboard.

All dried fruits can be added to chutneys to replace some of the sugar content and to add color and texture. Whole raisins, for example, will make a very dark, rich chutney, somewhat lumpy in texture because some of the fruits stay whole. Whole dried apricots will cook down to a thick, light orange purée (page 113).

Fall's apples and pears are still available and in good condition throughout the winter months.

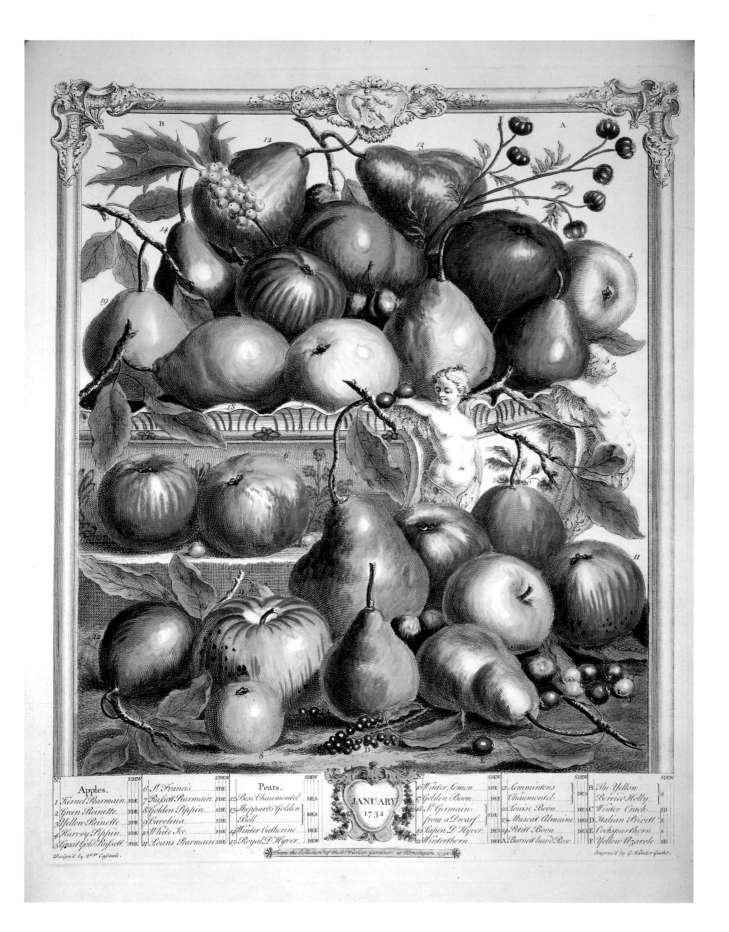

Fresh oranges brighten up winter days. Pickle them whole or slices or use their juice and zest for flavor.

Western-style pickles, where crispy, uncooked main ingredients are steeped in spiced vinegar, whole raisins, currants, or golden raisins can be added to the jars to the advantage of flavor, texture and appearance.

Citrus fruits are all in peak condition during the winter. The juices and grated peels of oranges, lemons, and limes can all be added to chutneys and relishes and thinly pared strips of peel can give color and flavor to winter pickles. Oranges were not historically used as a pickling fruit. In the Western world, they were treated with suspicion until the seventeenth century and later were more often candied and made into sweet preserves, their savory potential going unrecognized. Sliced sweet oranges, however, make a delicious bittersweet pickle which is excellent with poultry and game (page 120). Seville oranges, the bitter type that are often used for marmalade, have a short winter season, usually around December and January. In most recipes that specify lemon juice, you can use Seville orange juice instead to give your pickle or chutney a light, bitter-orange flavor.

Small, soft citrus fruit, such as clementines and satsumas, can actually be pickled whole, using the same recipe as for orange slices (page 120). Be careful when choosing fruit for this purpose, that you find varieties with few or no seeds.

The smaller dried fruits are added whole to chutneys and the larger ones are usually chopped finely or ground before the ingredients are mixed. To make them cook down more quickly, all dried fruits can be soaked for a time before the chutney is made. The best way of keeping their flavor for the chutney and not throwing it out with the soaking water is to soak the fruits in the vinegar that you are going to use in the final making.

DRIED FRUITS

In the Middle East, dried fruits are made into pickles in which they constitute the single main ingredient. They are soaked in vinegar and then cooked with spices and flavorings to a purée, making the end result really more like a chutney than a pickle in texture. In more

WHOLE FRUITS

Both lemons and limes can be pickled sliced or whole (page 116). They can also be chopped up very finely and added to chutney mixtures. There are recipes for pickled whole lemons that date from the eighteenth and nineteenth centuries and which have changed very little over the years. The process begins with slitting the lemons into quarters but

keeping them joined at one end, and then packing them with salt. There are various methods for covering them with spiced vinegar, brine, or oil, processes that you will find in books of Middle Eastern cooking today.

Citrus fruits can be bought well in advance of using and will keep for several weeks in a cool, dry pantry, but, as with all fruits, the sooner they are used the better they will taste. The skins of most citrus fruits are waxed and so, if you are pickling them whole or unpeeled, it is best to scrub them before using.

Fresh cranberries are another winter specialty. They ripen in the fall but soften and mellow in the winter frosts to be ready for converting into relishes for the Thanksgiving turkey. Cranberries keep exceptionally well. They are usually sold vacuum packed and as such will keep in the refrigerator for up to one month. Frozen ones can also be used. Pineapples and bananas are available all the year-round in most countries, but, in the northern hemisphere at least, they are at their best in winter.

Pineapples have been regarded as such an exotic fruit, that there are few pickle or chutney recipes for them, at least in Western cookbooks (page 125). The attitude has been that a pineapple should be appreciated in its natural state. However, pineapple relishes are popular in Southeast Asia, there are Indian recipes for pineapple chutney, and John Evelyn, writing in England in the seventeenth century, recommended pineapple as a fruit for pickling, although he did not give a recipe. The pineapple is a refreshing fruit and contrasts well with hot curries and other spicy foods. It will keep for up to a week in a cool, dry pantry or cupboard.

Bananas have a soft, creamy texture and sweet flavor that makes them ideal for chutneys (page 114). Add a little orange, lemon or lime juice and you have a perfect combination. In India and the Middle East, mashed banana with lime or lemon juice, spices, and yogurt makes a quickly prepared relish or sambal to go with warming, spicy foods. Use bananas that are ripe but not over-ripe. The skins should be a good bright yellow but without any brown patches. Store them in

a cool, dry place for up to two days.

Another popular sambal ingredient is coconut and it always tastes better used fresh (page 118). To prepare a coconut, first remove the tufts of coarse hair. Then pierce the "eyes" with a skewer and let the liquid drain into a bowl. Place the coconut on a firm surface and hit it firmly with a hammer all-round the middle to make the outer shell split. Remove the shell, cut the inner flesh into pieces, and cut away the brown skin. Then grate the flesh, either by hand or using a food processor.

VEGETABLES

Most winter vegetables can be turned into some sort of savory preserve. Crunchy celery and Florence fennel were both popular pickle ingredients in the eighteenth and nineteenth centuries. They make light-flavoured, crisp pickles, and relishes (page 122). Both red and white cabbage can be pickled and, in Germany, white cabbage is made into a fermented pickle called sauerkraut which can take up to a month to prepare and which is served with salted meats and sausages.

Of the root vegetables, carrots, beets, and turnips are the most used, and rutabaga can be put into chutneys. Carrots can be pickled raw, either sliced or in thin sticks. In some older recipes, where they are the single ingredient, they are boiled until they are tender before being put into the pickling vinegar. Beet pickle has always been a popular inclusion on the cold table. In the eighteenth and nineteenth centuries it was valued as much for its color as for its flavor and it was used as a garnish for salads and cold meals. Turnip pickles and relishes are not so popular in the West but are quite common in the Middle East and well worth trying.

In the nineteenth century, many American country homes had a root cellar, where home-grown root vegetables were stored from fall to the end of winter. Now, however, our houses are too warm. Root vegetables are best bought when you need them and stored in a cool place for up to one week. The best way we have, in fact, of storing vegetables, is to make them into winter preserves.

LEFT: Beets can be made into jewel-colored pickles and quickly prepared relishes.

Apple *and* Date
Chutney

Dark and thick, this farmhouse-style chutney is hot, spicy, and sweet. For a bittersweet chutney, replace 4 ounces of the dates with chopped candied peel. Leave the chutney for at least two weeks before opening. Unopened, it will keep for up to two years.

FILLS FIVE TO SIX 1-POUND JARS

2 pounds pitted dried dates

4 onions (about 1 pound)

4 large cooking apples (about 2 pounds)

½ cup packed dark unrefined sugar

½ cup black treacle

2½ cups cider vinegar

1 tsp salt

1 tsp cayenne pepper

1 tsp ground allspice

Finely chop or grind the dates and onions. Peel, core, and finely chop or grind the apples.

Put the chopped dates, onions, and apples into a preserving pan or nonreactive saucepan. Add all the remaining ingredients. Bring slowly to a boil, turn down the heat and simmer, uncovered and stirring occasionally, for 1¼ hours, or until the mixture forms a thick, dark chutney.

Spoon the hot chutney into warm, sterilized jars and seal immediately.

APRICOT, CARROT, *and* RUTABAGA
CHUTNEY

~

The pieces of rutabaga and carrot remain slightly crunchy giving this hot, light-flavored amber chutney an interesting texture. It is ready to eat after two weeks. Unopened, it will keep for up to one year.

FILLS ABOUT FOUR 1-POUND JARS

1 pound dried whole
*   apricots*
3¾ cups white vinegar
5 large carrots (about
*   1 pound)*
1 small rutabaga (about
*   1 pound)*
4 onions (about 1 pound)
1¼ cups Demerara sugar
2 tsp ground mace
2 tsp cayenne pepper

Soak the whole apricots for 12 hours in half of the vinegar. Drain and chop them, reserving the vinegar.

Peel and finely chop the carrots, rutabaga, and onions.

Put the chopped apricots, carrots, rutabaga, and onions into a preserving pan or nonreactive saucepan with the sugar, mace, and cayenne pepper. Pour in the reserved and the unused vinegar and bring slowly to a boil. Turn the heat down and simmer slowly, uncovered and stirring occasionally, for 1 hour, or until the mixture is soft and thick.

Spoon the hot chutney into warm, sterilized jars and seal immediately.

PICKLED BEETS *with*
HORSERADISH

~

The deep red of this unusual, spicy beet pickle is flecked with the lighter color of pieces of horseradish. Fresh horseradish is sold throughout the winter and jars of prepared horseradish are sold year-round in supermarkets. If you are lucky enough to obtain fresh horseradish, scrub it well and chop it finely in a food processor rather than grate it by hand, which is a slow process releasing unpleasantly pungent fumes. Leave the pickle for one week before using. Unopened, it will keep for up to six months, but once opened, it should be eaten within one week.

FILLS ABOUT FIVE 1-POUND JARS

3¾ cups white-wine vinegar
2 tsp allspice berries
2 tsp black peppercorns
2 pieces blade mace
2 tbsp juniper berries
12 whole beets (about
*   3 pounds), uncooked and*
*   scrubbed*
6 ounces horseradish,
*   grated*

Pour the vinegar into a nonreactive saucepan and add the allspice berries, black peppercorns, mace, and 2 teaspoons of the juniper berries. Bring slowly to a boil over low heat. Remove the saucepan from the heat, cover, and leave for 2 hours. Strain.

Boil the beets whole, in their skins, for 45 minutes, or until they are tender. Drain, then peel and dice them while they are still warm.

Crush the remaining juniper berries, either by using a mortar and pestle or with the handle of a heavy knife.

In a bowl, mix together the beets, horseradish, and juniper berries. Pack the mixture into cold, sterilized jars. Pour in the cold, spiced vinegar to cover and seal immediately.

PICKLED RED CABBAGE *and* CARROTS

~

Floating strands of carrot add orange highlights to the overall crimson-purple of this crunchy, savory pickle. Leave it for four days before using. Once opened, it should be eaten within one week. Unopened it will keep for two months.

FILLS ABOUT SIX 1-POUND JARS

1 red cabbage	1 tsp cloves
2 to 3 carrots (about 8 ounces)	1 tsp mustard seeds
	1 tsp allspice berries
3 tbsp salt	1 tsp black peppercorns
3¼ cups white vinegar	4 pieces blade mace

Finely shred the cabbage and cut the carrots into julienne sticks. Layer the cabbage and carrots in a bowl with the salt. Cover and leave for 12 hours, shaking the bowl occasionally.

Pour the vinegar into a nonreactive saucepan and add the cloves, mustard seeds, allspice berries, peppercorns, and mace. Set the saucepan over low heat and slowly bring the contents to a boil. Remove the saucepan from the heat, cover the vinegar, and leave until completely cool.

Drain the cabbage and carrots in a colander. Pack them into cold, sterilized jars. Strain the cold vinegar and pour it into the jars to cover the vegetables. Seal immediately.

BANANA *and* RAISIN CHUTNEY

~

The flavor of this light brown chutney dotted with dark raisins is sweet, dry, and spicy. Ready to eat after two weeks, unopened, it will keep for up to one year.

FILLS ABOUT FIVE 1-POUND JARS

12 bananas	1½ tbsp ground cumin
6 onions (about 1½ pounds)	1½ tbsp ground cardamom
2 cloves garlic	2 tsp ground coriander
1 tsp salt	1 tsp cayenne pepper
grated peel and juice of 1 large orange	2½ cups white-wine vinegar
3 cups raisins	

Peel and very finely chop the bananas and the onions. Crush the garlic with the salt.

Put the chopped bananas and onions with the crushed garlic into a preserving pan or nonreactive saucepan. Add all the remaining ingredients and mix together. Set the saucepan over low heat, bring slowly to a boil. Simmer for 1¼ hours, or until the mixture is thick.

Spoon the hot chutney into warm, sterilized jars and seal immediately.

Pickled Red Cabbage and Carrots

FIG CHUTNEY

~

Dried figs are extremely sugary and make a dark, rich, and sweet chutney. Leave it for at least two weeks before using. Unopened, it will keep for up to two years.

FILLS ABOUT TWO 1-POUND JARS

3¾ cups white-wine vinegar	2 pounds whole dried figs
2 tsp black peppercorns	2½ cups Demerara sugar
1 tbsp allspice berries	1 tsp cayenne pepper
1 tbsp cloves	2 tsp ground cinnamon
	2 tsp ground mace

Pour half of the white-wine vinegar into a nonreactive saucepan and add the peppercorns, allspice berries, and cloves. Bring to a boil, then simmer, covered, for 5 minutes.

Strain the vinegar into a large bowl. Put in the figs and leave them for 2 hours. Drain the figs, reserving the vinegar, and finely chop them, removing the small piece of stem from each one.

Pour the reserved vinegar together with the unused vinegar into a preserving pan or nonreactive saucepan and add the chopped figs, sugar, cayenne pepper, cinnamon, and mace. Bring slowly to a boil and simmer for 1¼ hours, or until the mixture is reduced to a thick paste. Stir frequently as the figs reduce into a very thick purée.

Spoon the hot chutney into warm, sterilized jars and seal immediately.

LEMONS *and* LIMES *pickled in* OIL

~

The unlikely combination of ingredients produces a bitter pickle that is surprisingly good with rich, spiced dishes. As the lemons and limes are used whole, buy unwaxed fruit; if you cannot find any, scrub well before using. Leave the pickle for three weeks before using. Unopened, it will keep for up to three months. Once opened it should be eaten within a week.

FILLS ABOUT FOUR 1-POUND JARS

6 lemons	2 tsp coriander seeds
6 limes	4 bay leaves
4 tbsp salt	8 dried chili peppers
2 tsp allspice berries	3¼ cups sunflower oil

Scrub the lemons and limes and slice them thinly. Put them into a colander and sprinkle them with the salt. Leave for 24 hours, then drain them.

Pack the citrus slices into cold, sterilized jars, sprinkling a few allspice berries and coriander seeds in each jar. Push one bay leaf and two dried chili peppers into each jar. Fill the jars with the oil and seal immediately.

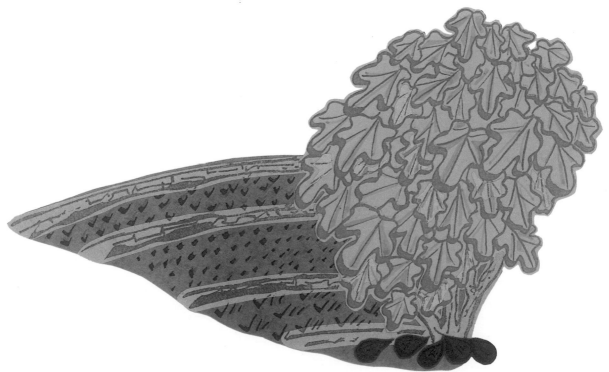

YOGURT *and* COCONUT

Creamy, refreshing, and extraordinarily simple to make, this is the perfect relish to accompany a curry and counteract its hotness. Buy an unwaxed lime; or scrub the fruit well. The relish will keep for up to 24 hours in a covered container in the refrigerator.

MAKES ABOUT 1¼ CUPS

1¼ cups packed freshly grated
   coconut
1 small onion, very finely
   chopped (optional)

grated peel and juice of 1 lime
½ tsp cayenne pepper
½ tsp ground cumin
4 tbsp plain yogurt

Mix all the ingredients together and leave them to stand for at least 2 hours before serving.

SWEET ONION *and* LIME RELISH

Vinegar is not used in this relish composed of softened and browned onions coated in a sweet-and-sour sauce. Instead, all the necessary acidity is supplied by the limes. Buy unwaxed limes; if you cannot find any, scrub the fruit well. The relish will keep for up to one month if stored in a covered container in the refrigerator. Bottled, it will keep for up to two months.

FILLS ONE 1-POUND JAR

3 large onions (about 12 ounces)
grated peel and juice of 2 limes

2 tbsp dark unrefined sugar
½ tsp cayenne pepper
2 tbsp sunflower oil

Cut the onions in half lengthwise. Thinly slice each in half crosswise.

Put the sliced onions together with all the remaining ingredients into a saucepan. Cover, set over high heat and bring slowly to a boil. Turn the heat to the lowest point so the onions are just simmering and cook slowly for about 1 hour, stirring occasionally, until the onions are soft and brown and the mixture is dry but not too sticky.

Leave to cool and serve. Alternatively, spoon the hot relish into a warm, sterilized jar and seal immediately.

ORANGES *in* HONEYED VINEGAR

Bittersweet orange slices steeped in a mild honey vinegar are excellent with game and poultry. Leave the pickle for one week before using. Unopened, it will keep for up to six months. Once opened, it should be eaten within one week.

FILLS ABOUT FOUR 1-POUND JARS

10 sweet, juicy oranges, *seedless if possible*	*1 cinnamon stick*

2½ cups white-wine
    vinegar
	1 small piece dried gingerroot,
	    bruised

scant 1 cup honey	*2 tsp cloves*

Scrub and thinly slice the oranges, removing any seeds. Put the orange slices into a nonreactive saucepan and pour in enough water to just cover them. Set them over low heat, bring slowly to a boil, and simmer for about 40 minutes, or until the peel is soft but the flesh is still intact. Lift out the oranges using a slotted spoon. Reserve 1¼ cups of the liquid.

Pour the vinegar and the reserved liquid into a nonreactive saucepan. Add the honey, cinnamon stick, gingerroot, and cloves and bring to a boil. Add the orange slices and simmer, uncovered, for 15 minutes, or until the peel becomes slightly translucent.

Using the perforated spoon, transfer the orange slices to warm jars. Boil the vinegar liquid for 5 minutes longer. Remove the cinnamon stick and gingerroot and pour the hot, spiced liquid over the oranges, allowing an even number of cloves to fall into each jar. Seal immediately.

RAW CRANBERRY RELISH

~

The uncooked fruits give this deep crimson relish a refreshing, bittersweet taste. It is a seasonal accompaniment to turkey, roast meats and game. Thawed frozen cranberries can be used if fresh ones are unavailable. The relish will keep for up to one week in a covered jar in the refrigerator if you do not add the chopped orange until just before serving.

MAKES ABOUT 2 CUPS

2 large oranges
1⅓ cups cranberries, fresh or
  frozen and thawed
2 tbsp red-wine vinegar
2 tbsp sunflower oil
1 onion
½ tsp ground allspice
¼ cup sugar

Squeeze the juice from one of the oranges and cut off the peel. Pour the juice with the peel into a food processor. Add the cranberries and red-wine vinegar and work them to a rough purée.

Heat the oil in a skillet over low heat. Add the onion and allspice and cook for about 3 minutes until the onion is soft. Add the sugar and stir until it melts.

Add the onion and sugar mixture to the cranberries in the food processor and process again to a purée. Pour the mixture into a bowl.

Cut the peel and pith from the remaining orange and finely chop the flesh. Mix the orange flesh into the cranberry mixture.

Serve the relish chilled, on the day that it is prepared.

CHRANE *with* RAISINS

~

Chrane is a Jewish relish made of beets and horseradish that is usually served with corned beef. In this version, the addition of raisins introduces a sweeter quality. If you are using fresh horseradish, scrub it well and finely chop in a food processor rather than grate it by hand, a slow process which releases unpleasantly pungent fumes. The relish can be eaten on the day that it is made, but it will last for up to a week in a covered container in the refrigerator. In a sealed, sterilized jar, it will keep for up to three months.

FILLS ONE 1-POUND JAR

2 beets (about 4 ounces),
  uncooked and with skin
6 tbsp horseradish,
  grated
3 tbsp raisins
6 tbsp red-wine vinegar

Boil the beets whole, in their skins for 45 minutes, or until they are tender. Drain and peel them, then finely grate them.

Mix the grated beets with the grated horseradish, raisins, and red-wine vinegar.

Place the relish into a covered container and leave for at least 4 hours before serving. Alternatively, spoon it hot into a warm, sterilized jar and seal immediately.

CHINESE PICKLES

~

Made with brine instead of vinegar, this interesting mixed vegetable pickle is crisp and light. Leave it for four days before using. Unopened, it will keep for up to one month. Once opened, it should be eaten as soon as possible.

FILLS ABOUT TEN 1-POUND JARS

⅓ small white cabbage
  (about 1 pound)
4 white turnips (about
  1 pound)
1 head celery
1 cucumber
6 dried chili peppers
6 thin slices fresh gingerroot
1 tsp black peppercorns
½ cup salt
4 tbsp Chinese rice wine
  or dry sherry

Finely shred the cabbage. Scrub the turnips and peel them if necessary, then cut them into small, thin sticks. Cut the celery into 1-inch sticks. Cut the cucumber into quarters lengthwise and then into 1-inch pieces.

Spread the prepared vegetables on clean, dry dish cloths on a tray. Cover them with more dish cloths and leave for 3 hours to dry.

Put all the remaining ingredients into a nonreactive saucepan together with 1¾ quarts water and bring to a boil. Turn the heat down and simmer for 5 minutes, then remove from the heat. Leave to cool completely, then strain, reserving the liquid.

Pack the vegetables into cold, sterilized jars. Pour the cool liquid over them to cover and seal immediately.

Celery *and* Fennel Relish

Rather like a hot salad, this vegetable relish can be served hot as well as cold. Eat it on the day of making, or store it in the refrigerator in a covered container for up to three days.

MAKES ABOUT 1¼ CUPS

4 large stalks celery	*4 tbsp olive oil*
1 small head fennel	*juice of ½ orange*
1 small onion	*2 tbsp white-wine vinegar*
1 clove garlic	*2 tsp Dijon mustard*

Finely chop the celery, fennel, onion, and garlic.

Heat the oil in a skillet over medium heat. Put in the finely chopped celery, fennel, onion, and garlic and cook them for about 2 minutes, stirring, until the onion begins to look transparent.

Stir in the orange juice, wine vinegar, and mustard and bring to a boil.

Remove the pan from the heat. Transfer the relish to a small dish and serve hot or chilled.

PINEAPPLE *and* GINGER
CHUTNEY

More syrupy than most chutneys, this hot-and-sour version is nevertheless thick enough to hold the pineapple chunks prettily in suspension. Ready to eat after two weeks, unopened, it will keep for up to six months.

FILLS FOUR TO FIVE 1-POUND JARS

2 large pineapples
2 tbsp salt
4 ounces fresh gingerroot
10 cloves garlic
1¼ cups packed light soft brown sugar

1 tsp ground cinnamon
1 tsp grated nutmeg
2½ cups white-wine vinegar
2½ cups golden raisins

Remove the skin from the pineapples. Slice and then finely chop the flesh, removing the cores. Put the pineapple pieces into a bowl, sprinkle them with the salt, and leave for 1 hour. Drain them.

Peel and grate the gingerroot. Peel and crush the garlic cloves. Alternatively, peel and roughly chop the gingerroot, put it into a food processor with the garlic cloves and process until they are very finely chopped.

Put the sugar, cinnamon, and nutmeg into a preserving pan or nonreactive saucepan. Pour in the white-wine vinegar and bring to a boil. Add the pineapple, ginger, and garlic with the golden raisins and simmer gently for 2 hours, or until the liquid has reduced and thickened to a syrupy consistency; it will be more runny than the usual thick, puréed type of chutney but will thicken as it cools.

Spoon the chutney into warm, sterilized jars and seal immediately.

Acknowledgements

Key – (a) above   (b) below

Murray Alcosser/Image Bank 6–7, Bodleian Library 8 (a), Nick Nicholson/Image Bank 8 (b), e.t. archive 9, Gabe Palmer/Ace 12–13, Paul Thompson/Ace 14, Hulton Deutsch 15, Mansell Collection 16, e.t. archive 17, Vibert-Stokes/Ace 18, Robert Opie 19, Pictor 20–1, e.t. archive 22, Robert Opie 23 (a), Michael Freeman 23 (b), Michael Freeman 24, Vibert-Stokes/Ace 26–7, Pictor 28, Charles Mahaux/Image Bank 29, Robert Opie 30, Mansell Collection 39, Michael Freeman 42–43, Bodleian Library 44, e.t. archive 45, Mauritius/Ace 46, Tangent/Ace 47, Mauritius/Ace 62–63, Bullaty/Lomeo/Image Bank 64, e.t. archive 65, Bodleian Library 66, e.t. archive 67, J. Allan Cash 82, Anand Razdan/Ace 84–5, David W. Hamilton/Image Bank 86, e.t. archive 87, Trevor Wood/Ace 88, Carol Kohen/Image Bank 89, Michael Freeman 106–7, Lesley Howling/Ace 108, e.t. archive 109, Pictor 110, Bodleian Library 111
All other photographs are the copyright of Quarto Publishing plc
All illustrations are the copyright of Helen J. Holroyd
We would also like to thank Elizabeth David Cookshop, The Piazza, Covent Garden, London WC2E 8RA for supplying equipment used in photography.